FINDING
REALITY
BEYOND FEAR

Rev. Marilyn L. Redmond
BA, CHT, IBRT

EARTH STAR PUBLICATIONS

FINDING REALITY
BEYOND FEAR

Rev. Marilyn L. Redmond

EARTH STAR PUBLICATIONS
Eckert, Colorado
First Edition
First Printing February 2018

ISBN 978-0-944851-53-1

Dedication

I dedicate this book to Macklin Van Wyk, who has given me his constant love since I met him over 16 years ago. His support, honesty, integrity, and loyalty offered me the ability to grow beyond my fears and past traumas. I was loved enough to move into a life that is indeed incredible. With this loving and stable foundation, I finally was able to rise beyond my history and into a life of unconditional love.

Prologue

Welcome to FINDING REALITY BEYOND FEAR. This book relates the chronicles of my moving through many problems into the solutions that worked for me. In this book I wanted to share my process and progress while advancing from fear, resentments and guilt of the past and releasing them. Learning I could replace difficulties, shortcomings and negative behaviors for a better life were a new idea for me. The more I let them go and replaced that space in my new consciousness with love and grace, the more my life improved over time. I found myself living in grace at times and wanted my whole life to become so calm and lovely.

I hope you find my adventures and experiences helpful and encouraging on your spiritual path, too. Instead of "poor me," I now live in the light. It meant that I could change my energy from the lack of light to ascend into a higher consciousness of love and light.

Becoming fearless was not my goal at first, but in faith, I do not have fear; I was "reborn." Rather than seeing the right and wrongs of others with criticism and judgment, I now see that love is all there is. *Returning home* means releasing my human faults and reclaiming my Christed inheritance. We are all born in the image of God's spirit. My heart opened. I found God within my heart to fill me and to share with others. Everyone has love within that brings us together into the one spirit of the universe.

Throughout my journey, I did not know I was moving into reality, maturity, and becoming an adult. The pains of growing up and spiritual growth disappear in a new understanding and realization. The reward of being free of the ego and moving into my heart has brought joy, gratitude and being in the presence of oneness.

Table of Contents

Part One
FINDING GRACE

My Search for Answers Begins 9

My Bubble Bursts 14

Life is a Choice 18

An Inner House Cleaning 22

Sorting the Truth from the False 27

Only Love is Real 31

My Path to Maturity 35

Transforming from Victimhood to Strength. 38

Forgiveness Brings a Gift 42

The Present Moment 47

I Am in the Genie in the Bottle 50

A New Life 54

Part Two
FINDING BALANCE

Getting On With Life 59

Living More Fully 62

The Secret For Reality 66

One Bite at a Time – Keep it Simple 70

"Easy Does It" is Changing Me 74

First Things First 77

Think 80

This Too Shall Pass 84

Let It Begin with Me 88

St. Francis of Assisi Prayer 92

Part Three
FINDING SANITY AND HEALTH

Truth about Alcoholism and Drug Addiction 99
Treat Violence as a Disease 104
Domestic Violence Has a Spiritual Answer 110
Bipolar Disorder is Not Forever 121
Love Brings Sanity to Mental Illness 131
A Simple Way to Raise Your Consciousness 136

Part Four
FINDING TRUTH

Letting Go of Fear is Faith 141
Changing My Life into Gold 145
What is Innocence? 170
A Spiritual Master Lives in Christ Consciousness 177

Epilogue 185
About Marilyn L. Redmond 187
Publications 189

Beyond Denial

By Marilyn Redmond

*Why this painful life that never seems to end? Why
don't my knees release their rigidity? What's
the issue that reminds me, I am separated from God? Is it denial
of sexual abuse or rape throughout my life? Or, is it anger
since my mother could not care for me? Deep, depressing
energy blocks God's love and stops its flow from head to toes?*

*Thick barriers, walls of protection from devastation, trapped in
childhood dread, prevents maturity. It's time to open Pandora's Box
and let the enemy out. Shine on light and love by opening my heart,
clearing the remnants away. Now space remains for love to fill
the hole within. A healing occasion with joy and reality.*

*Time to replace the path of emotional pain, replace with
truth in its rightful place. God's love endured
throughout old times. Being grateful brings love divine.
Willing to see the wisdom learned, expands my spirit
for daily joy, brings love and light forever more. My past no longer
has a hold on me. Only happiness, serenity in eternity.*

PART ONE

FINDING GRACE

My Search for Answers Begins

Is your life unmanageable, miserable, or just frustrating? My life became a search for answers because of my traumatic past. I read countless biographical books, looking for an explanation and a way out. I listened to the experts in medicine, church, school, and any place I thought would help. I found the answer and life is not a mystery anymore. Follow me on my discovery of what works in my life.

I felt powerless and I looked for ways to influence my circumstances, in order to achieve a better outcome. I had been trying to control my life to be safe. Some people call it putting your ducks in a row. I did all the right things, I thought. Somehow, my row of ducks fell apart and I was not happy with the results. I worked at this for many years. I finally had to admit that I was powerless over my life.

I tried to please my parents. I was obedient. I tried to achieve good grades in school and my parents still did not acknowledge me. When I graduated as Valedictorian, they did not celebrate all my hard work or offer congratulations. I always sat first chair flute in the orchestra and bands, but I was still not acknowledged at home. I thought when I soloed with the symphony; finally, my parents would applaud my efforts, recognize me and my ability. However, my achievements did not bring happiness or support. The harder I tried to line things up, the more they came apart.

Finally, I realized that trying to change others to be what I wanted was not the answer. In fact, the more I tried to make my life go right, the more miserable I became.

I successfully masked my despair and stuffed my feelings. My superficial façade was not detected. However, my miserable inner life was painful and I felt dejected. I thought if I teach, marry, and have a family, then I could create a happy family. I spent thirty years playing this game.

I had not recognized how well I was playing the role of victim. I always reacted to the threatening experiences around me. My life trauma started in childhood. I reacted to events and circumstances, trying to protect myself from my mentally ill mother, alcoholic father, and caustic stepfather. Later in my search for answers, I realized that I married a man who mirrored my family. Those traits were familiar to me and I fooled myself, thinking he could change.

I did my best to look good to others. We appeared to be a happy family in our community. My husband ran our printing business and I was a teacher. I took our children to church; we were involved with community affairs. I had a clean and organized home. Our yard was always mowed and weed free. Our landscaping was full of beautiful flowering shrubs. We took lovely trips, even out of the country to exotic places. I pretended everything was fine, while in reality my home life was a mess.

On the surface, everything looked like I had the perfect life. Why then was I so miserable? Why was my marriage a battleground? Why did our children have problems at school? Why didn't I have friends? I wanted to be happy and enjoy my life, but these were only fleeting moments in a stressful life. This was such a mystery to me.

Was I really creating more chaos and turmoil when I was only trying to bring cheerfulness to my family? I was the passive director of the show, but no one stayed in their designated role. I did my best to be pleasant, kind and caring. I thought my family members were the ones with the problem. We went through our routines, but no one was enjoying life. Why couldn't I have a happy family? Why was I powerless over my family? If they just did what I wanted, our family would be wonderful.

Getting honest with myself created a major change in my attitude. I had come to believe in a life that was terrible, horrible, and awful from my dysfunctional and abusive childhood. I was reenacting my childhood with my family. I was compensating for my loss of not being nurtured while growing up. I had a glimmer that perhaps I was not supposed to be in charge of others. Maybe, they had their own lives to live.

Unconsciously, I was reacting to everyone, trying to keep myself safe. I thought I was a loving mother; however, I found that my fearful growing up prevented me from opening my heart to send real love to my household. They were looking for the same love I wanted from my parents. I was playing the same role as my parents in my family. I did not love myself and realized that meant I could not love others.

I needed hope. Was it possible to overcome the conditioning of my cruel youth and domestically violent marriage? I learned from my church to stay in my marriage, and my psychiatrist gave me prescriptions for anxiety. If I continued to listen to them, I would stay in a marriage of tragedy and fatality. I had to find new answers. My only hope was to change my approach from reacting from my past terrifying experiences to finding a safe place where I could open my heart for feeling real love.

I had been living in fantasy and illusion. This is a form of

11

insanity. I wasn't being honest with myself. Without honesty, there is no sanity. I had to admit that my life was not sagacious. It almost killed me. It brought me to try suicide and my husband tried to kill me several times.

I wanted out of my prison of fear. Moving into a life of reality was my only hope. I needed to find a higher power of love to replace my fearful mind. I had to change from being a fear-based person into a love-based person. I needed a design for living.

I vowed to be as honest as I could be, so I would not be insane like my mother, a paranoid schizophrenic. Realizing that I cannot change others did improve my life; I accepted the responsibility to change myself. Launching into unknown waters, I began my search for truth.

My Dream

My dream to move out of strife, abuse, stress
has finally come. Releasing all resistance. I'm
no longer numb, feelings flow, the frozen iceberg
has melted to experience Joy.

Safe at last in the arms of God, Love protects
Me and abounds. Surrounded in serenity filled
With Joy for eternity. Harmony abounds forever,
Balance brought this peaceful place.

Out of fantasy, illusions, the past,
Future worries disappear only security
Remains in the presence of God.

Kindness rules the day, helping others in dismay,
find their way. My needs are met, life is good.
Grace surrounds me manifesting spiritual fruits.

Instead of knowledge, Ego, the brain,
My heart has opened and life's in place.
The fears dissolve in the sunlight of
truth. Only a beneficent loving, caring spirit is there
to embrace forever more.

My Bubble Bursts

The only way for me to break away from my family was to go to college. I met a fellow there my first day; we were both studying to become music teachers. During our dating, I realized he had a temper. Nevertheless, I was drawn to his charming personality. We married, and I believed I could help him heal from his harsh childhood; I believed I had enough love for both of us. I thought I could "fix" him. Years later, I realized he had the same characteristics as my family.

As a child, I loved the song "Someday My Prince Will Come" from the Disney movie *Snow White and the Seven Dwarves*. It was my wish growing up. When I was in grade school, I would play it on the piano and sing my heart out. I was going to find my Prince Charming.

I also enjoyed a radio show called "Let's Pretend." These imaginings led me not to see the reality of my life. This is called denial. I was not acknowledging the reality of my life. I was lying to myself and I did not recognize it.

As I got older I pretended my life was fine, when down deep I was not truthful with myself. I thought I deserved to be punished; that I was not "good enough." I believed that if my mother was hurt nightly, I was no better than she is. I deserved to be treated like my mom. I pretended that I could save myself by saving her. This brought constant stress and vigilance through-out my life. It wasn't until years later that I realized I never felt safe or protected.

I always did what I was told. I got good grades to prove to my family that I had value. It gave me a sense of worth. Straight A's in school did not impress them, but nevertheless, they became my mask. I never caused any trouble for my family.

I did not have friends or fit in with groups. I was in bands, orchestras, and youth groups, but I felt left out and not part of the groups. I studied harder, practiced my flute more, and did the yard work around the house to show everything was going well. Unknowingly, I had become a walking robot without feelings and desperately wanting people to acknowledge me. I looked good to everyone, while I was dying inside.

Was I insane? Yes. I was not living in reality. I finally had to break the bubble of fantasy and get authentic with myself. After thirty years in my abusive and dangerous situation, I learned I had to wake up. Year after year, I kept doing the same things repeatedly, expecting different results. This is a definition of insanity.

Somehow, I found myself in the family I thought I left from childhood. I had created a marriage that copied my parents; not the happy family I knew I desired. My Prince Charming was not so charming. I had ignored and disregarded the futility and fatality of my situation. I had not escaped my childhood abuse, it had only become worse.

I could no longer live in the desperation of being threatened for my life. Without any answers to my predicament, I tried suicide. I felt hopeless and helpless. It was live or die time. I prayed to be in a better place. Angels came to help me during this time of despair. This brought my accepting spiritual help to move out of my predicament. I found there was a heavenly power that cared for me and could help me. There was a better way.

I read a quote by Albert Einstein, the legendary scientist,

"We cannot solve our problems with the same level of thinking that created them." I started to understand that my life was motivated from fear. I was the great victim. I even won an international writing contest with my article, "All Time Victim." I had been in hell and the only way out was to move up into a loving solution.

Fearful motivations create dreadful results. With no mindful thoughts, only fearful ones, my life was a disaster. Thinking my decision might be the wrong one, my inaction was not working either. I needed to make a choice and take action. I was irrational and my outcomes were irrational. Everything I did was from fear.

Finally, when I realized that I was not honest with myself, I saw why my life did not work. I was a scared little girl in an adult body. I had gone to church all my life, but I was not connected with God. A lack of faith was keeping me insane, hopeless, and helpless. I did not understand faith.

Not trusting God was a major issue for me. I found that my ego was running the show in my mind, which projected my fear-driven life around me. Learning that my Ego's fear is powerless unless I give it power was profound. This meant I could release my ineffective negativity that kept me powerless. I had to change my life into loving behaviors and thoughts for loving consequences. Cause and effect became real to me.

I started to take an inventory each evening to see if I had been selfish or generous, dishonest or honest, frightened or courageous. My list grew with more self-searching to identify and change my thoughts and efforts for the next day. I found that replacing the self-pity I learned from my mother with gratitude created a huge shift in my life. When I started directing my life from the fruits of the spirit listed in the Bible, I started to feel better. I was merging into conscious contact with a loving higher power.

My bubble of protection had kept me from reality. My fear-based life had caused me to stay in a depression, bleak and dependent. I found a great relief in the information that said I could walk out of my Ego's messages. I had been hiding from life, trying to be safe, because I did not deserve good things. Living in these lies of the Ego kept me imprisoned.

I could open the door to this prison and leave. I felt hope for the first time. With new information, my fears started to melt. A friend told me there is always hope. Fear comes from the lack of information.

When I substituted the positive for the negative, the bubble burst into feeling good. Ultimately, my new love-based life gradually opened into the unlimited prosperity of the universe. My old emotions progressively left and new good feelings replaced them. I became honest, open-minded and willing to change into reality.

Life Is a Choice

How do you trust people who are into their own problems and ignore you? I could not rely on my parents because I saw them fight nightly. I decided I would not grow up and be like them. I assumed God was not there for me; I was not good enough. Being naive kept me ignorant. I did not understand life. How do you trust something you cannot see?

I was not born into a family that was rich in emotional balance and wholeness. My parents did not accept me with unconditional love in an environment of security. I did not know how to trust. My image came from going to church and looking good with my perfect attendance pin from Sunday school. That would pull me through life. My parents could not model what they did not have.

My best thinking kept me in a prison of fear and survival. My mother married during the Great Depression and her advice to me was "you marry for the man to take care of you." Marrying my college sweetheart turned out not to be sweet. I had turned my life over to him. He was harming me physically, mentally, emotionally, and spiritually.

I had to get real. The night I believed I would not get home alive from a Canadian vacation with my husband, I prayed, "God, please help me, I really don't want to die." I thought that if I were perfect, I would not be hurt; however, my life did not seem to advance that way. My drunken husband pulled off the road, passing out over the wheel. I felt relief from his manic driving. I left a message for help at the restaurant, where we stopped for coffee in the morning. Five police cars showed up to my cry for assistance. I called my son. He picked me up and drove me to my minster's home, where I would feel protected.

Events unfolded that led me to find a wonderful organization for friends and families of alcoholics. My husband called me and explained that good wives of alcoholics go to Al-anon. I had never heard of the group.

Wanting to be a good wife, I went to my first meeting that evening. This was something new to me. The members were laughing and having a pleasant time. They said, "Keep coming back," so I did. Hearing that I was insane surprised me as I had seven years of college; however, I knew my life was unmanageable. I always tried to look faultless, which I thought gave the appearance of being successful in my teaching career and as a wife and mother.

I found a woman to sponsor me through the program. She informed me that I was sicker than most of the women and sent me to a family treatment program at a local hospital. While there, I found myself staying longer as I learned that I was addicted to prescription drugs for my anxiety. The instructor said, "One drink and one pill is six times the effect."

The first night of inpatient treatment, I was exploring the steps for recovery from addiction from the prescriptions instead of my addiction to my husband. While in the hospital bed, I realized I had been in hell. The only way for me was up. I realized if I turned to a loving power for help and to take care of me, I could move up and out of my misery. This seemed like a wonderful idea. Neither my family nor my husband had acted as if they cared for me. It seemed like a great answer.

In treatment, I was told toxic substances are poison to the body. Therefore, the prescriptions were aiding my demise in addition to my husband's actions. My body told me I was dying. In addition, I found that mind and mood altering medicines had stopped my emotional growth. I had not grown up.

The light had gone out of my life. I felt a small glow barely remaining inside. I was in a hopeless and desperate place. My misplaced reliance and loyalty on family ironically built a strong bonding while I was looking for the missing love.

Because my parents were not available, I looked to others. However, all family members had their own dysfunctional ways and were not necessarily emotionally available. Sometimes, there are healthier members of the family like aunts, uncles, or grandparents to turn to. If so, then you are fortunate.

Finding a husband did not work, either. My husband was also needy, abused, and lonely. Emotionally, we were two little scared children. It became necessary for me to make a decision and take action if I wanted to live. It was time to move beyond survival.

I had to find a divine source to sustain me through the walk out of my darkness, disease of addiction, and hurt. From my experience, it is not possible to mature beyond this type of relationship without a Higher Power. I chose to focus on my powerful source that could love me, no matter how terrible and worthless I felt.

Discovering that it is necessary to connect consciously to this positive power was a little bewildering. If I did not set up the circumstances, what could happen? Reluctantly, I had to let go of the outcome. Understanding that I did not have faith was a major revelation because I went to church my whole life. Learning I could not have fear and faith at the same time became a big change.

Through experimenting with faith, I found partial faith

brought partial results. When I decided not to limit myself, I resolutely took a leap of faith. The results that manifested from 100 percent faith bloomed better than I could have predicted. The future is full of infinite possibilities waiting to happen.

I was ready for a better life. It was time to open my heart and get out of my head; to walk away from fear and the abusive past. I realized love is a choice. I preferred to turn my life over to a loving Heavenly Father for unconditional love and emotional security. Over time, my old ideas about God evolved into a positive energy source that supports me in all things. Today, a power greater than me streams through me, bringing the best solutions and resolutions.

Being in the presence of God has become the most important thing in my life. Embracing faith and trust brings better results. Recently my inner voice told me, "You are part of it; you are a part of the love in creation called 'God.'"

An Inner House Cleaning

Turning to a higher power to care for me and keep me safe was a novel idea for me. As a child, I thought of the God from the Bible stories and pictures of him in a white robe. Other children in my Sunday school class told of their wonderful adventures, and I knew that would never happen to me. I felt I was not good enough for him to help me. In addition, I did not know how to pray; in my understanding prayers came from the hymnal at church or the minister. One summer in Vacation Bible School, I memorized the 23rd Psalm, but I did not understand it.

One night when I was very young, scared, and watching my parents fight, I instinctively prayed for God to help me. I did not want to be beat up like my mother or abused again. I did not know how to pray, it just happened. Many years later, I had an experience as an adult in the middle of the night; I believed I would die from a car ride with several near head-on collision misses. Again, I intuitively prayed, "God please help me; I really don't want to die." I needed a God who would love me unconditionally.

Shortly after that, I found spirituality in 12 Step Programs. They encouraged me to pray and meditate. This seemed foreign to me. Why would I pray? At home I was taught not to ask for help and my church preached against meditation. Apparently, this prayer for God to help me was heard. I am still alive. Surprisingly, classes, counseling, and other information became options for me to learn new ways and how to involve myself with my spiritual growth.

Through attending meetings and reading the material, I found that God and Love are within. I never heard this in church, and it made sense to me now. I have learned that when I have negative emotions, thoughts, or communications, they stop my connection to God, also known as my Higher Power. Through prayers and meditation manifesting my guidance and direction, I have now a faith and trust in God's love that I could not see in the past. I had to clear away the negative and fearful barriers preventing my ability to feel good.

As I became more in tune with my inner-self, through prayer and meditation, I began to realize there was an energy protecting and keeping me safe. I almost died twelve times. My angels, guides and masters were there with me each time. I have always had invisible help; I just was not aware.

Through faith, I have changed my perception to an inner power of love that is always with me. I began to have feelings of fullness and self-worth; I am no longer lonely or insecure from my horrifying past.

The answer was to become mindful that my job was not to search for love, but to find all the barriers within myself that stop a loving energy. Finding the truth inside meant I had to remove the obstacles of false beliefs. I also had to remove all my negative thoughts, emotions, communications, and behaviors. I had to sort the truth from the false. Through this inner house cleaning, I removed everything that covered the truth of the *Great Reality* within. These old ideas and emotions were barriers to my happy life.

Doing this required me to list my fears, resentments, and unconstructive ways that prevented the awareness and my acknowledgement of a loving force. The more I identified each anger or resentment, the more I became calm and less upset with others and myself. Ultimately, I found that anger is a childish reaction when one does not get their way. It is like throwing a temper tantrum. It was time to release all my anger and rage and accept that the circumstances, people, and harms were necessary so I could move beyond my immaturity. That was the past. I could now let go and give them to God. They were my lessons teaching me to grow up.

When I was teaching, a weekly newspaper came for the children that listed fears and the ages that you usually outgrow them. I was reminded that I needed to list every fear to release them all. It was time to move into faith. I could not have fear and faith at the same time. It has been said that fear is "False Emotions Appearing Real." I found that fear comes from the ego and stops me from moving into the presence of my higher power's love. It is an illusion; like a mirage, fear keeps me irrational.

Evaluating each resentment and fear, I found I was seeing my adult life through the eyes of a three-year-old child. I stopped growing emotionally when my dad beat my mother. I had never grown beyond because of the fear of physical harm. I had never grown up. I looked like an adult, but inside I was a terrified little girl.

If I do not let it go, my fear will come back for me to face. After several years of releasing most of my fears, I had a major one surface. I was in Seattle when my car was stolen, while I was speaking about my near death experience to a group that studies near death experiences. Some hoodlums took my car, damaged the leather seats, left the odor of marijuana, and abandoned it out of gas. Shortly after that, I left for a two-week trip. A week later, when I was in Paris to see the Spiritual Sights of Mother Mary, I received a call from the police. They found the car which was a mess and in disrepair. I told them where to tow it and I contacted the insurance company when I returned.

In a meditation, I was told that I had attracted the experience from the energy of fear that my car would be stolen and I would be left without transportation. Fear attracts the very thing for which you are afraid. Like the statement, "What goes around comes around." There is a universal law that says, "Like attracts like." I had released many fears at that time, but I had forgotten about my fear of the car being stolen and leaving me stranded. This helped me realize that I had more fears to release, as I no longer wanted to attract what comes with them.

My recent and last significant fear to overcome was to go up in the huge Ferris wheel at the waterfront in Seattle. It looks out over Puget Sound, the ferryboats, and the Olympic Mountains. When my friend first asked me to go with him on the Ferris wheel ride for his birthday, I explicitly said, "No."

I had had a hysterical experience in a carnival ride called the Octopus in sixth grade. The ride was stopped immediately, so I could get off. I vowed never to go on a carnival ride that ascends again.

After talking with my spiritual teacher, I realized I could go into meditation and change my fear to faith. This changed my feelings, and I agreed to go. I comfortably went up in the ride as if I were in the arms of God's protection. At the top, a magnificent orange sunset filled the sky as it reflected off the water and the buildings behind us. I was in Joy! This picture is the cover of my "ultimate self-help book," *Paradigm Busters, Reveal the Real You*, available on Amazon.com. The orange sky on the cover of the book represents Christ Consciousness, which signifies fearlessness, unconditional love, and maturity.

Becoming Fearless

What is fear?
Where does it come from?
Why do we have fear?
Is fear beneficial?
Why is it detrimental?
What are emotions and feelings?
Can they be changed?
What are vibrations and feelings?
How does cause and effect work?
What is Illusion?
What is reality?
How do you move into reality?
What stops reality in life?
What are the biggest obstacles?
How can I move into reality?
What is acceptance?
What is forgiveness?
What is karma?
What is responsibility?
What is sanity?
What is heaven on earth?
What is the 5th dimension?
What is Christ-consciousness?
What is a Master?

Sorting the Truth from the False

In my journey to search for answers to improve my life, I learned to acknowledge the problem. I needed hope and faith to move forward in life. The next step was to have courage to proceed with my inner inventory; I was ready to move into a better understanding of my life. I had never been open to anyone about my abuse and being a victim. I thought if I revealed these things, no one would be my friend. I am sure others figured this out, but I was not honest with myself.

I had never shared my secrets with anyone. This was a difficult situation for me. I was afraid that you would not "like me" if you knew what went on at my home. My anxiety of opening up to what I carefully hid for so many years was overwhelming.

Living in my past harms was familiar and I was taught not to spill the beans. I did not know who I was. However, I learned to face my fears when I found a higher power that would love me no matter what surfaced from my past.

It became necessary for me to tell the truth with no pretending or hiding the real story. It was essential for me to find a safe person who understood my breaking through to release my lack of reality. I had to separate the truth from the false. This was scary because I would no longer look good by wearing a mask. I had had conversations with my higher power about how awful my life was. I fearlessly wrote out my faults and difficulties from fears and resentments; however, to tell a person was another story.

Fortunately, I found enough courage to open up and expose

my hurts and harms of growing up and from my marriage. It was the right time to start my journey of honesty, with me, another person and with my Higher Power. When my friend shared her own story and understood my plight, I was able to see a different perspective on the situation.

Through this encounter, I learned that every time I point a finger of blame for my problems towards another person, there are three fingers pointing back at me. I had participated in each event and I had a part in it. If I was blaming others; I was not seeing the real picture. I actually was giving my power to them. I had to take responsibility for my part.

A bigger picture enfolded when I began to understand where I had been selfish, dishonest, fearful, and inconsiderate. I had to look at my side of the street. Looking at my faults was a new awareness. I have a favorite quote from *A Course in Miracles*. "Your task is not to seek for love, but merely to seek and find all of the barriers within yourself that you have built against it. It is not necessary to seek for what is true, but it is necessary to seek for what is false."

My survival had created a selfish person by using others for my security. I was looking for love in all the wrong places. I found that my dishonesty was largely with myself. As a child, I reacted in fear, but as an adult, I have a choice to respond more appropriately.

My fear came from continuing emotionally to act as a child, avoiding physical hurt like my mother experienced. In doing so, I was actually being inconsiderate of myself, by acting in my immaturity. I could no longer use others to be there for me. I gave my power to everyone else to take care of me.

It was time to grow up. I could release my fears as I moved into faith. My new journey was into the light, where the darkness of fear is gone. When I am in the present, there is no fear. The more I understood that I could outgrow all my fears and move forward in a new adventure, the fears from the past faded. I could choose to walk in faith.

I had been reacting from my harmful history or worrying about my future. My worry about financial insecurity was an illusion. I always had eaten and had a roof over my head. Fortunately, through all the difficulties, I was able to pay my bills. I had taken on my mother's fear of lack of money from her growing up in *The Great Depression.*

Sorting out my fears frees me to be present in my current experiences. My feelings of lack of love and security kept me in an emotional prison. I was still alive, even though I had almost died many times. I can open the door, walk out of that mindset, and move into the feelings of love of a heavenly spirit that was protecting me all the time.

Releasing the past and future trips from my head was a gradual victory. I no longer needed to listen to my brain's messages that kept repeating from events that had no meaning anymore. I learned tools to handle those situations with loving solutions as forgiveness, compassion, gratitude, and unconditional love.

Understanding that I wrote my life's script to move my energy out of the fear and into unconditional love was a new piece of information. These people played their parts for me to have the opportunity to find forgiveness and change my life to love. When I thanked them in meditation for playing their parts, I became free.

Finally, my inner peace can happen. I can forgive my parents totally. I am able to forgive everyone in my life from the past, present, and future, including myself. I needed to forgive the world and forgive God. This was a huge leap of faith for me to trust in a spirit of loving energy and not people. It became obvious to me, I am writing a new script for my life using affirmations of truth, knowing I am safe today.

The consequences of this change of focus mean that I can now experience serenity rather than conflict. I know how to focus on love rather than fear, guilt, and shame. I can choose to be a love-finder rather than a fault-finder. I am capable of being a love-giver instead of a love-seeker. I am able to transform into being love.

Only Love is Real

After sharing with my trusted friend, my life became more smooth and pleasant for a while. It was a relief not to have those burdens on my shoulders. I could relax and have less apprehension until my angers and resentments surfaced, again in different ways.

Making a choice to release my burdens and troubles was new to me. The feelings and emotions that I had allowed to run my life disconnected me from belonging. When I deny myself, I deny the love within. Every time I see myself as "not good enough," in lack, or insufficiency of any kind, or not safe, I am in denial of the real me. Thinking that it is humble to deny my talents and abilities, I really deny the divinity within.

Resistance to change kept me doing the same thing over and not questioning if there was a better way. Deciding to move out of my previous thinking threatened my family. However, my acceptance of the truth ends my denial. Most people are not into self-examination and inquiring. Therefore, it became important to find people who support my new ideas and purpose. My friends and jobs changed.

However, realizing that I did not need anger to cover the fear was a new understanding. It was time for me to acknowledge I had anger, even rage. In my early years, children were to be seen and not heard. In addition, the unspoken message was nice little girls do not get angry. Stuffing my anger about my mistreatment was safe. When I was younger, there was no communication or feelings in our home. I suffered in quiet desperation.

However, now my resentments became obvious. Not only were my fears an obstacle to my prosperity and new life, but so was my anger. Listing them and seeing how staying angry with others gave them power over me, I realized I was reacting and staying a victim. I began to see that these people or situations were dominating my life. It was time to finish cleaning house.

I found that anger comes from my perception. I could see myself angry because I was not getting my way, I did not like the way others were acting or living their lives. Moreover, I was not happy about the way my life was going. It became necessary to accept people and situations the way they are. They are living their lives as they choose. It is not my responsibility to direct their lives for my benefit. The resentment was like a temper tantrum. This is immaturity.

How was I going to release my anger? I bought some helium balloons and wrote the names of the people with whom I was angry on each one. I let them go up into the sky until they disappeared. This letting go was a relief.

Some resentments were not leaving easily. I learned to pray for those people. I prayed for what I wanted for them. Health, prosperity, happiness and wellbeing were being sent in my prayers to those people. I did this for two weeks. I found I felt differently about the people as I was praying for them. However, several prayers took longer than two weeks to change my attitude towards those for whom I was praying.

The change surprised me. I felt compassion, forgiveness, and unconditional love. It made sense. They came from the woundedness that they endured in their lives. I did not feel victimized, but empowered with my new perception. I found gratitude that they played their parts so well that I had to transform my attitude for peace of mind.

Another helpful piece of advice was to find a way that I might be helpful to them. This brought us together. Seeing where I could be helpful created a new relationship. I never thought I would see these people in an accepting way before. However, by forgiveness, I gave up the past emotional chains to release them for a new day of our being compatible.

Accepting people, places and things as they are is not always easy, and I did not have to like the way it was. There is a slogan, "Live and let live." I just had to accept the reality of it and grow up. That I had to accept life as it happens and not the way I want. I need to meet life on life's terms and move ahead.

Interestingly, after taking an inventory of my interactions with others, I found I was inconsiderate of myself by playing victim to all these old immature thoughts. Releasing them, making amends where appropriate, and forgiving them and myself was important. Then the past would no longer be the motivation of my actions. Breaking my habit of reacting could bring positive outcomes.

The solution of changing my energy from being upset or disappointed about the situation was amazing. Surprisingly, I could move my feelings from being upset after a time to being disappointed. When I became disappointed, it seems the feelings faded.

I am powerless when I am in denial. When I accept everything, I can then change it. Acceptance places me in power. I am responsible for my feelings. I am responsible for my life. If I can change my beliefs, I can change my actions; therefore, I can change my feelings. Old feelings can change and pass, thereby allowing space for good feelings to fill the new void. "This too shall pass."

"There are in truth no incurable conditions," said Edgar

Cayce, the Father of Holistic Health. A shift in perception from fear to love—living instead of dying—made the difference. As time progressed, continuing my self-analysis became necessary to grow into maturity.

Being honest with myself, it became obvious that my old thinking was irrational. It had to be; how else could you justify my erratic behavior? If you read a dictionary definition of rationalization, you will find that rationalization is giving a socially acceptable reason for socially unacceptable behavior and socially unacceptable behavior is a form of insanity.

Today, I can gain a new perception and feel like I can master my emotions instead of reacting from them. Stopping to give myself a moment to act appropriately instead of the old rash reaction is life changing. I then can let go of the anger. Spiritually, I know that I created these situations for my growth. I take responsibility for them, today. I have created a new foundation for my new life.

My Path to Maturity

As I progressed in my expedition into reality, it became clearer that my Ego had been running my life. Some people say ego stands for "Edging God out." I also saw this as "my will be done." Earlier in my life, I never actually took the time to analyze what I was doing. I automatically went through my life without any forethought. What I learned at home, school and church was my information.

Today, I have learned to turn within for my direction and guidance. This produces better results. I move from insanity to sanity, from old ideas into truth. If my ego's fear is running the show, then I will have baleful, irrational results. When I come from my heart and inner wisdom, my life goes well. It is about cause and effect.

Realizing that resentments covered my fear, I was ready to release my childish reactions and move into forgiving the people and situations. This allowed me to emotionally move out of the past harms and hurts.

Over time I realized that fear is like a bogeyman. It is akin to the child in bed at night who thinks there is an ogre under the bed. The parents turn on the light and there is no monster. Both emotions — anger and fear — are reactions from a frightened child. It was time to finish my inner house cleaning.

I chose to release my fears one by one. As I humbly requested each identified fear to leave, I replaced the space with love and grace. While on a camping trip in Death Valley National Park, I was meditating. For the first time in my life, I felt grace from head to toe. It felt wonderful. It was the beginning of more experiences in a happy direction.

This change surprised me. I felt empowered with my new understanding of a bigger picture. I transformed my feelings for peace of mind. Walking through my fears and releasing my view of being badly treated in the past has brought me into a new life. I see the folly of buying into them. They seem to disappear as I allow myself to move forward in faith. "This too shall pass" is a popular saying to move forward.

Resentments and fears had stopped me from receiving miracles in my life. As I let them go, good feelings filled the empty space. Currently, surprises and miracles are popping into my life, because the love is finally able to manifest.

Currently, I am enjoying more grace. My compulsive behavior has stopped. Needing to survive has turned into thriving. Abundance and prosperity has replaced my feelings of lack and not enough. I feel safe, secure and loved. When I moved from an ego, fear-based life into a love-based life, I found a new foundation. for my life. I found that I am responsible for my life and my feelings. With faith, I can move forward and enjoy what life has for me.

Learning that I can only change myself was a novel idea. When I respond to life's challenges with a loving solution, I can pass on the love of the universe to my family, friends and others. I feel joyfulness and in harmony. Becoming a conduit of love was not my intention when I started this journey, but I like my improved life. Giving to others has become a treat for me. I am aligning with the spirit of love, *Thy will be done*. Moving up the ladder of consciousness is becoming an adventure. The cause has changed and the effect is terrific. There is one more important part of the process before good orderly direction becomes a reality for me. Next, I eat humble pie.

Love Heals

Who knows what's deep
Inside needs
to surface? An inner
housecleaning to find
intense pain, to be revealed.

Days and years persist, as
forever. Pills only mask
hurt, stop the search. One
brave day end all medicines
and trust divinity

Resistance brings more
suffering through times
of anguish, strife,
despair. My body cries
for help from anywhere.

Gnash, a monk, answers my
cries. Help from Tibet
arrives, his messages
bring great, powerful relief.
Sadly, more pain continues.

Years of silently, emotionally
protecting my son from harm.
Finally, accepting, releasing
in love, brings peace. Finally
over, time to move on.

Transforming from Victimhood to Strength

My path to a better life brings new ideas and understandings different from my background. I learned that self-honesty is the best policy. I had to come out of denial and fantasy by acknowledging that my life was really a mess. I thought I was a great manager, believing this would keep me safe from traumatic situations.

As I began my new journey into honesty, I found that when I walk in faith the results are better than when I tried to arrange the outcomes. Today, I do my necessary steps for my mission while leaving the total results to the universe. Surprise, I found the outcome is great. It is better than I could have planned.

A tough part for me was to acknowledge that I have to identify and change my mindset and behaviors from being fear-based into loving solutions. How could I not be a good person? I took care of my family, taught school, went to church, and I worked in the family printing business on my off hours from teaching. I had not looked at how my needing to survive and protect myself was not working. I had left myself out of the picture of taking care of me.

My motivation was not from love, but endurance and need. In my past, I saw myself as a wonderful person, who was there for everyone. Realizing my life was actually based in fear and fantasy was life changing. I was not there for me. My real dreams were left in the dust while I was there for everyone else.

Interestingly, the more I release my negative emotions, thinking and responses, and replace them with my new healthy ways of accepting conditions without judgments and criticisms, the better my life improves. I move from functioning in the problem to focusing on the solution.

It has taken years to identify and release my old thinking, emotions and reactions into healthy, loving communications and good feelings. The work has been worth it. My book, *Paradigm Busters, Reveal the Real You,* has the steps I took to transform my life. I feel better about myself and those around me.

My world is turning in a new direction. Continuing on my path of fresh beginnings, I found I still needed to make amends to those I had harmed. It was not my nature to harm a person. However, I had taken a few things that were not mine when younger, for which I made an apology and restitution.

Moreover, I found my negative emotions did harm others. I could not love my family if I was full of fear. Fear stops love. I was not that wonderful person when my emotions were not allowing my love to flow to others.

I made a vow to myself not to place myself in harmful situations, again. In meditation, I was told to treat myself like a princess, because I was the daughter of the Creator. I was learning to love myself so I could pass this on.

I have spent years cleaning out my channel of old negative thoughts, words and actions to allow a creative, loving force to project outward. How do you make amends for this? I discovered that changing myself to being a loving, healthier person, they did receive the missing love; this made the difference. I changed. I became a new person in their lives and I wanted to emit love. I was living my amends.

It took eighteen years to feel the feelings of my side of my domestic violent marriage. Unwittingly, I participated; I was not the victim and he the bad person. Subconsiously, my trying to defend myself from harm was like an attack on my husband. It was as if I took out a subconscious gun and shot him in trying to protect myself. Unknowingly, I was attacking him. This hurt caused him to react observably to harm me back. The passive-aggressive game intensified over time. My side was not seen and his trying to protect himself was unrecognizable. We were two little children trying to make it, but hurting each other in the process.

I could no longer make him out to be the awful person. This was a huge admission. At one point, I wrote an apology from my side of the conflicts and sent it. I was as much at fault. This served me well when, several years later, I was invited to our twin grandsons' high school graduation.

At first, I was not sure I was emotionally up to it. However, with many years of growth on my new path, I was able to attend the festivities and be brave. For the 48 hours of celebrations and the ceremony, I was able to be around my ex-husband and not play the victim. This was a huge victory for me. I cleaned my side of the street and I was free.

I just heard last week that he died. I knew him for 60 years and we were married for 30 years of that. It upset and touched me more than I would have guessed. I had not seen him after our divorce, except for our grandchildrens' graduation. My grief blindsighted me these last few weeks. I am better understanding the dynamics of how I never grieved many parts of my life, so I could completely leave the past behind.

Today, I am glad that I had the courage to own up to my part of our difficulties and now grieve them, too. God bless him! I see how sad it is when two people do not know why they are having problems and do not search for ways to resolve their conflict. He became my teacher to find the inner changes I needed for me to become forgiving, be in gratitude, compassionate and have unconditional love for him.

In my prayers and meditation, I have thanked him for being in my life today. I can walk away with a clean heart. My weaknesses have become my strengths. I am empowered. Finally, I am at peace and in serenity. Surprisingly, I learned this is maturity. I was told I am taking the high road. My reward is that I am free of my history and ready to live in the "Now." I am happy to have a healthy life today.

Forgiveness Brings a Gift —
Leaving the Past Behind

There is always more to learn on the path of spirituality and personal growth. I will never graduate. Nevertheless, I realized after the benefits of forgiving my ex-husband and acknowledging my part, I wanted to move into this better place in all my affairs. For that reason, I discovered that forgiveness and making amends frees me to do this. Learning that inner peace is only by complete forgiveness, I have to forgive all those who have been harmful to me in some way, though this is not easy for me.

How could all those people be forgiven when I was harmed by their actions or comments? However, I read that *it is a spiritual axiom that every time we are disturbed, no matter what the cause, there is something wrong with us.* This means I have to look at myself and get honest about my motivations and actions.

It is necessary to look at my side of the street in all my dealings. I have to see where my own behavior has affected someone else. The picture is not pretty when I get honest. Realizing how selfish I was in trying to protect myself and survive was not easy to accept. I used people for my security, protection, to love me, and take care of me. It is time to grow up.

I was dishonest with myself, thinking other people were there to make me okay, provide my needs, and love me. I was so afraid in my victim place that all I could see was poor me, poor me. I recognized that I was keeping myself that victim by not acting in my own best interest.

Becoming assertive instead of passive was the key to changing my thinking from being the injured party. It was a huge step out of my playing the victim. Taking the steps to become courageous to speak up for my needs had never been in the cards for me. When I was a child, I was to be seen and not heard. In fact, my stepfather told me, "We do not want to hear what you have to say."

My trip sorting out the truth from the false is continuing. This is a long process with lots of challenges and lessons in its path for not to mentally and emotionally continue recreating my mindset. I vowed never to volunteer to be a victim again. In addition, I learned to forgive myself as I did survive the abuse and difficulties. Now it is time to move into maturity.

I was living in a fantasy that everyone and everything should go my way. I needed to give up the past by leaving it emotionally behind and move into "The New Me." This is one of my early poems in my first book, *Roses Have Thorns*. This clears the slate to live in the "Now."

Vision – A "New" Me

Total acceptance of myself means the opportunity
For reality. Unconditional love grants
My own gentleness, caring. Courtesy lifts
my dignity, sees value. Tolerance
understands favorably my mistakes,
errors. Self-esteem believes in confidence,
guides my life. Sharing my experiences, feelings
creates life's happiness. Many interests
bring a fulfilling life helping others
through their strife. Spirituality generates
peace of mind, worth, knows
the purpose for my birth.

43

Today, I accept life on life's terms, knowing that reality is now and everything is exactly as it needs to be. It is no longer necessary to defend myself. The change is how I will respond in the situation with a loving solution for you and me. Determining the loving response for others and me brings a great sense of ease because I align with the flow of the universe.

The biggest lesson and most difficult to accept is the truth about all my difficulties, toxic people, and harms. I came to realize that this is frequently called karma. I created my past and it came back for me to correct in loving and positive ways. All negative energy has to be offset by a positive solution. It is called balance.

I had to balance my not so wonderful past with improved actions, emotions and thinking. Edgar Cayce, The Father of Holistic Health, said, "For without passing through each and every stage of development there is not the correct vibration to become one with the creator." Another quote of his is, "Thus the individual does not go to heaven, or paradise, or the universal consciousness, but it GROWS to same." This told me I was on a trip to grow into knowing that there is one spirit of love.

If I want to grow into the peace that is not of this world, I have to offer complete mercy to all the people, events and things in my life that cause difficulties and challenges. Compassion and forgiveness allows love to return to my awareness. I will see a world of peace, safety, and joy.

Experiencing this loving energy of spirit that is in all of us and sustains us was an awakening. These people and circumstances were actually giving me the opportunity to change my fears, resentments, shame and guilt into seeing the love below the appearance. They provided the opportunities for me to become so upset that I was willing to give up my selfish, self-centered ways to move into compassion, forgiveness, gratitude and unconditional love.

I can love the person and not the behavior. They were acting out what needed to be changed in me. They actually were giving me the chance to purify my own soul. My old projections from karma can transform into loving my neighbors as myself. We are all one in grace.

This week I had the occasion to turn karma into grace. Blindsighted by a person with very unkind judgments that gravely upset me seemed like the end of the world. Once again, it felt excruciating and unsettling. I felt attacked at the very core of my being through thoughtless condemnation. However, after the emotional fire died down, I knew enough to find the source of the difficulty and painful feelings.

As I sorted out where this pain originated, I realized this was a part of my hidden self that still needed to be resolved in love. The intellectual knowledge was ready to become an emotional shift to end the past feelings. It was time for this old energy to leave.

Discussing this with a trusted friend, I discovered the exact nature of my problem. Immediately, I felt the "bitterness" of my stepfather and his mother in the environment where I was raised. Subconsciously, that energy was no longer needed with my better life emerging. I was not even aware that I still held bitterness.

What goes around does return. My new loving ways were pushing out the old for the new to replace it. It had to surface for my awareness and then leave. Finally, I was ready to handle the experience of the transformation. I could finally let it go and replace it with love and grace.

I can appreciate being in the "Now" and leave the baggage of the past that prevented the presence of love. Realizing he did me a favor with an emotional opportunity to feel and release the old harms brought relief. I am able now to be present in my life today. You might say it became a gift; one I did not expect, but was necessary. It feels like I have been born into a new energy by letting my past leave without condemnation upon the present. It's like receiving the gift of a new life living in the grace of universal love that sustains us all. My new year begins with leaving my past behind.

The Present Moment

Moving into the present or "Now" is fascinating. For many years, I prayed for a better life without the problems and hurts. Over the years, I learned to let go of past painful luggage and future worries for a daily pleasant mood. When I release fears and false beliefs, this makes room for inner love. Freeing those thoughts and ideas not aligned with love created the space where love can expand. This is often called growing up.

Facing my challenges, I found myself in a new place. Life around me seems different. I am not seeing issues around me in the same perception. It feels like I am not being caught up in the drama of politics, family or friends. It is a sense of being in the "eye of the hurricane," where it is calm. The winds are blowing beyond me; however, they are not affecting me.

I first recognized my new experience at my friend's family Christmas meal this year. They were his family and he would not miss their traditional Christmas morning brunch. In the past, members of his family were difficult, argumentative, and egotistical. It was not a comfortable circumstance for me. I was in a room of people where I was not part of the family; I felt out of place.

However this year, I was present, feeling composed, pleasant and easy instead of reacting to the drama as I had in the past. I didn't have the same negative feelings. Everything seemed neutral; however, they had not changed. It took me some time to realize it felt like serenity.

I found myself emotionally moved away from my judgments

of the past, to accepting each person as they are. The issues were dissolved and gone. This new space was pleasant, but unfamiliar. I had changed by not reacting to their games, problems or controlling ways. I had moved into being current. Could I do this with the rest of my life?

The circumstances that arise from these relationships are the very faults in me that I need to heal with the love and forgiveness within. I know today that those situations outside of me are a representation of what I need to heal in me. This understanding formed a new me; I was my own foe.

Today, I have self-love. I do not need them to love me, take care of me, or keep me from being lonely. My inner spiritual awareness is alive and well, taking care of me better than anyone does. Finally, I am content with me.

When more old emotional problems surfaced from my side of the family, I found I could place myself in the calm center again. Seeing those who had been upsetting to me in the past was providing me with another issue within myself to heal. This time I released the anger and expectations. Everyone is exactly where he or she is supposed to be in his or her experience. Understanding that they are being themselves, and it is not my job to change them, is emerging in my life.""Live and let Live" is a slogan that I finally understood.

It comes from within; not from others. If I focus on what I am doing and just send forgiveness, love or acceptance to those around me, I am acting mature. This peace surpasses all understanding. I have now joined the realm of spirit. I establish a conscious contact with my inner spirit to keep me in the present.

Surprisingly, I found myself in grief. Feeling grief is new to me, too. Letting go of the old me was bringing up sorrow for the past leaving and dying. However, I like the idea of my previous feelings leaving.

The earlier issues are no longer a concern. I am detached from my miserable past of people and situations. I came into a feeling of being in the world. but not of it. Now, I am free to be myself and enjoy life. Lately, I am watching funny movies because laughter is good medicine.

This suggestion from Mother Teresa is a great help to maintain empowerment, sanity and success. It was found on the wall in Mother Teresa's home for children in Calcutta.

People are often unreasonable, irrational, and self-centered. Forgive them anyway.

If you are kind, people may accuse you of selfish, ulterior motives. Be kind anyway.

If you are successful, you will win some unfaithful friends and some genuine enemies. Succeed anyway.

If you are honest and sincere, people may deceive you. Be honest and sincere anyway.

What you spend years creating, others could destroy overnight. Create anyway.

If you find serenity and happiness, some may be jealous. Be happy anyway.

The good you do today will often be forgotten. Do good anyway.

Give the best you have, and it will never be enough. Give your best anyway.

In the final analysis, it is between you and God. It was never between you and them anyway.

I Am the Genie in the Bottle

My journey into a new awareness has not been easy. I was told, "Growing up is not for sissies." Tough times still manifest on my path. The journey continues today with my trials and tests; however, I have tools now to go through them and no longer run from reality.

Finding a conscious contact with my higher power was my answer. One great benefit is that my depression, Bipolar Disorder, many addictions, and history of abuse are no longer a concern. When I am daily in the presence of God, there is only light, joy and gratitude. This allows clarification into my awareness. This became the basis for moving out of mental illness, domestic violence and a dysfunctional lifestyle. Honesty is my connection to a higher power. I got honest with myself and moved out of the darkness.

The lack of light and love stopped the flow of healthy energy throughout my body that caused my sicknesses. Moving into the light is the solution to my medical and relationship problems. The barriers I had built to protect me were actually stopping good things in my life and health. The vital life force can provide the elements of health for the cells of the body to function appropriately. Supportive alternative assistance such as massage, chiropractic, and flower essences supports the flow of the vital life force to nurture my body and mind back to health.

These days, I found answers and now have enough self-esteem that I rise above dysfunctional gatherings, family, or circumstances. Today, it is possible to see a bigger picture by way of understanding with compassion and forgiveness. "To heal is to make happy" is stated in *A Course in Miracles*.

In the past, I listened to the authority around me and I was on my last legs. I was told to stay in a domestic violent marriage by the church and take the medicine by the doctor. I would not be alive today if I followed that advice. I can make myself happy and meet my own needs. This means I take responsibility for myself and respond in love for others and myself.

I learned to pray daily and meditate. Prayer is raising my focus into a higher consciousness beyond the ego. Then I am connected like tuning into the right station on my spiritual radio. Listening for the inner voice to provide guidance, knowing, or speaking to me is what I was missing in the past. My answers now come from within instead of the insanity around me.

Listening to the silent voice inside has given me directions and assistance in numerous traumatic situations. I could write a book describing at least a dozen life-threatening experiences. These have created a trust in God that I never had before.

Applying what I hear in meditation is vital. Once, while meditating at the ocean beach in Oregon years ago, I asked for instructions on what to do next. My spouse had abandoned me there at the end of our vacation. I did not like the answer at first and I asked for another one. It repeated two more times. I finally got the shock that I was to ask for a temporary separation. This was the most difficult thing to do at that time in my life. I was co-dependent and emotionally only three years old. I prayed continuously for 24 hours for courage to speak up when I flew home. If I had not asked for a temporary separation, I would not be writing this.

One evening, I heard the inner silent voice as my husband was approaching to beat me. I was told to pray, "God forgive him, for he knows not what he does," and added, "God bless him." Angels held him so he could not move toward me. After praying this twice, I was escorted by angels out of the room. He walked in the other direction to watch television in the family room. He never touched me again. This taught me to pray for my foe. I found that the presence of God is the safest place to be. No one attacks love.

I ask for "Thy will be done" and apply the guidance. This means I become a channel of love for others and myself. The Father and I are one. One day, I was thrilled as I had some extra insurance money from a car repair. In meditation, I was told it was for a friend leaving town on an airplane to another state. She was traveling to receive training for a new job without any cash for food. Surprised with the answer, I gave her the money. I find doing the right thing is never wrong.

In meditation, I am connected to the beneficent spirit that created the universe and supports me in all things. I find myself as part of the Creative Intelligence, Universal Mind, or Spirit of the Universe. I am omnipresent, omnipotent and omniscient. I am individualized consciousness. My new world came into view; all things work for good if you are on the spiritual path.

Currently, my abusive past is an old chapter in my history book. I now live through prayer and meditation to be a blessing to others and myself. I pray constantly to do the right next thing. With the guidance and help of a loving spirit, I act on my inner direction. I live without reacting to others around me.

Seaside Serenity

The ocean waves sound peaceful, silent, quiet,
calm, restful to my soul. Lullaby of tranquility
replenishes my woes. Time to stop
reflect, progress, and then reliance
on inner messages of grace.

Old emotions evaporate in the breeze. Replaced with new
feelings of joy, bliss, bring me to my knees
in gratitude, ecstasy. A new life emerges in the ethers
of purity. Reborn in unconditional love,
delight. Life's abundance, prosperity
is bright. Darkness, has left for the sunlight
of the spirit to shine, everlastingly,
eternally, within my mentality.

A New Life

Love waits on welcome, not on time, I found. With my brand new way of life, I have moved into a love-based life instead of a fear-based one. This has created a spiritual awakening. My lack of a conscious contact with a higher power was missing, even though I attended church for years. I found many things that were not supportive of the life that I wanted. A few of these I have shared throughout my stories. Socrates said, "The unexamined life is not worth living."

Through following the advice of "Trust God, clean house, and help others," I began examining my life. I have been scrutinizing my life for several years. As a result, I found that it was difficult for me to trust anyone, as my parents were not trustworthy. My marriage was full of domestic violence and with rape; it was not trustworthy either. How do you trust something invisible?

I discovered myself in perilous difficulties of life or death numerous times. It was obvious there was something there for me and it was keeping me alive. This became a faith that is strong today.

Recently, I fell down on asphalt in a parking lot from a hole that needs to be fixed. I got a black eye and my right arm, shoulder and wrist were injured and very painful. I fortunately had help to get up. Because I have arthritis in my knees, I would not have been able to get myself up. I luckily did not have any broken bones; however, I did break my glasses. The concussion put me out of business of helping my clients, writing, and artwork for several months.

Now, I am able to see the bigger picture of why it happened instead of blaming the church for poor maintenance. I found that some old energy still had to leave as I was in the old mindset, fearing being hit in the face since early childhood, when I witnessed my mother being beaten. I had also been fearful of a black eye in my marriage, which would have not been good when I went to teach at school. My black eye is healing and less purple each day.

I also found out reasons for having the concussion. One was to put space between my old life and new one. I was now able to stop being a workaholic and overachiever. My projects had to stop. I hope to resume soon with a realistic pace. It provided me with a vacation from work, which I needed.

I am still recuperating by resting, using ice on the painful parts, and allowing the healing to happen. I took the steps to get my glass frames replaced. I never thought about suing anyone. I responded appropriately. I was not happy, but I could accept this had to happen for my spiritual growth.

My early fearful energies needed to depart. This previous energy was being pushed out along with releasing other old negative energies. It was all part of my energy moving out as it is not who I am anymore. It was a necessary experience. It was needed for the new energy of love to have the space. Moving up the ladder of consciousness is my goal.

Life is about moving from being selfish to selfless. The film, *Ground Hog Day*, has become one of the acknowledged classics of American comedy. It is the story of a TV weatherman, Phil Connors, who is forced to live the same day, February 2nd, repeatedly until he gains some karmic—and comic—insight into his life. By the end of the movie, he has become less egotistical and more laudable. He has matured.

My task is not to seek for love, but merely to seek and find all the barriers within myself that I built against it. With over thirty years of cleaning and releasing, my fear-based negative thoughts, communication and behaviors from my ego; I have found a new me.

I do not think as a victim anymore. I have a sense of being worthy and assertive. I recognized that my childish eyes saw things differently from what they really were; realizing that my life is not what I thought, brought a new pair of glasses. With forgiveness, compassion, gratitude and feeling the presence of goodness within, I moved into a higher consciousness.

This allows me to help others from an elevated loving resolution for situations and old harms. My inspiration and training as a spiritual teacher, regressionist, educator, writer, counselor, and a medium are a few of my many gifts. They allow me to guide clients and readers of my books into positive solutions for moving forward in their lives. I am able to see beyond the observable into the root cause of situations, allowing loving resolutions. This ability resolves issues.

Today helping others is a big part of my life. The more I give, the more I have. My awareness of how smoothly my life is really going these days is amazing. Assisting others spreads a path before me that is calm and even.

I find the ultimate example of living a spiritual life is the activities of Mother Teresa. Mother Teresa was the founder of the Order of the Missionaries of Charity, a Roman Catholic congregation of women dedicated to helping the poor. Considered one of the greatest humanitarians of the 20th century, she was canonized as Saint Teresa of Calcutta in 2016.

It is necessary to seek for what is false and release it. I can leave fear, heartache and self-imposed boundaries behind. Instead, I am able to live a life full of purpose and joy. With my ego diminished, I can heal and be happy—I can reside in peace. With a sense of self-esteem and my needs met, I become a channel of help—I am an agent of love. I am able to be in reality, harmony, and in service.

PART TWO
FINDING BALANCE

Getting On With Life

"Let go and let God" is a saying that is popular today in many spiritual groups. It is a watchword to remind us that we are not in control of people or situations in our lives. Learning that I was not supposed to play God was new to me. I did not even know my actions were controlling to my family or others. My motivation was that if everyone is happy, then I could be happy and relax. I just wanted everything to come together, well.

When I first heard the phrase, "Let go and let God," it was almost earth shaking. How could everything happen appropriately, if I was not the coordinator? As a teacher, I managed my classroom very well. I was organized and the day went like clockwork. Additionally, parents came in to help the students with their studies regularly throughout each day. When I was the music teacher, I had taught the students every song, dance step, and instruments needed for each performance. I had produced many school programs and events, and every one was a big success. I knew how to get in there and make the pieces come together.

At home I had to be organized and have the projects completed on time to keep my husband happy. It was necessary to have dinner ready at the same time every night, or he would be angry. If we went camping, I was not to forget anything, or I would hear about it loudly.

I learned major lessons from trying to keep a marriage together that was not meant to last. It fell apart, even with all my efforts to plug the holes of the sinking ship. More efforts seemed to make things worse. No matter how hard I tried, my marriage was not working. I was frantic trying to keep the boat afloat.

Eventually, my husband and I needed to seek a separation. One afternoon, after a session with my psychiatrist, I realized that I did not have a workable marriage and my efforts were not bearing fruit. Letting go of my thirty-year marriage was traumatic. I would be abandoned. Now I understood that I had not grown up emotionally because of childhood trauma.

Our parting opened the door for me to have an opportunity to heal my life. I found opportunities to improve my self-esteem, attitudes, and unhealthy ways. While painting a portrait of an angel one night, I felt a new feeling. I had let go of the people in my life that I had hung onto for emotional support. The new feeling was the love in the universe finally being available to me. The people had stopped that love like barriers. I was now able to have a connection to the love of my higher power without the obstructions from my neediness. I never felt abandoned again. I was learning to allow love into my life.

I spent the next ten years learning to love myself and let God be my director and guidance. I gained self-love and self-confidence. I was learning to let love come into my life and heal the wounded parts of me to become a whole person.

I began the footwork to become the person I wanted for a companion. By now, I understood the law of attraction. My list for a new individual in my life was spiritual, honest, sincere, loyal, and trustworthy. In due course, little by little I changed to incorporate these qualities. I decided to join a spiritual study group called "Search for God" to help me grow.

When I was introduced to a man at the Search for God study group, I immediately knew that I would have a relationship with him. I attracted a man with the qualities I had listed, I realized during one of the meetings at my book study. I did not go looking for a companion. When I was ready for a new relationship, "he" appeared. He was the answer to my prayers.

I found the consequences were better than I planned. I had let God provide the person right for me. The universe brought him to me when I was ready for moving on with a partner in a healthy way. Sixteen years of unconditional love has been a real gift from heaven. Now with my spiritual growth, I understand that when the universe puts the final pieces together, there are wonderful results.

The real lesson came from learning faith and trust in a beneficent universe that wants the best for me. When I am allowing my faith to work, it connects with that force that knows what I need better than I do. I trust that the outcome is the right one for me.

Letting go does not mean giving up and it does not mean escaping into inert passivity. It means giving my struggle over to God and getting on with my life. I found that in letting go of my effort, I leave space for good things to manifest into my experience about which I might not have even known.

"Letting go and letting Go" has become a great tool for me. Life has become more effortless, graceful and pleasant. The more I let the universe determine the outcome, the better life goes. Maturity is a new consciousness for me. In fact, I know today that everything works for good for those that are on the spiritual path. I do not have to worry about the finale.

Living More Fully

Learning to live with the difficulties in life and give others the same opportunity was a challenge in my life. In fact, I was raised that people were supposed to all have the same thoughts and feelings. I had learned to postpone, trivialize, and sacrifice my life, without peace of mind because of the alcoholism and other dysfunctions in the family.

In my survival, I was controlling, fixing, and being a martyr. I learned this behavior from my mother; however, I was not aware of how this affected others for years. I was taught to deny myself the right to attend to my own needs, and then I denied that right to the people I loved. My mother modeled the behaviors that I performed well from a young age. It has taken years to undo the damage. For most of my life, I lived in a wilderness, depression and austerity, trying to go the way I wanted.

This existence was not productive in my marriage either. I was tied to my husband for security and love. He also was attached to me for his emotional refuge from his abusive childhood. Our co-dependent relationship went downhill over time.

At the turning point, I found a spiritual program that taught me how to reduce the effects of alcoholism, co-dependency, and mental illness in my family life. Finding programs with support and tools where I felt a warmth and acceptance was new to me. Discovering that I did not have life skills to mature, they offered the information I needed to move into a healthier place in relationships. I was to meet my own needs, validation, and love. I moved into recovery for co-dependency, alcoholism, and my other concerns. I had to focus on myself and take care of me.

That was a surprise; I had tried to change my husband for years. Over time, I realized that I was powerless over others. In The Serenity Prayer, it says that I need "the courage to change the things I can." It was my journey in life and if I became unselfish, my life would change. I did not know I was selfish; I called it survival. I found out I could only change me.

I learned to trust in a Power greater than myself. Instead of thinking my husband was to take care of me, I found a higher power that loved me unconditionally. My new understanding of God cleared the way to change my dependence on my husband, family, and others.

The past was not enjoyable, and I was ready to turn my life and will over to a Higher Power and use spiritual tools to guide me in my new adventure. Over time, I found that I was not alone because those in my study group were learning like me. My Higher Power and support group had never left me. I only needed to open my heart so my love could manifest in my life. I pushed through my denial of enabling and need to control. I learned that no situation is hopeless. It had not been safe to be open-hearted. Learning that life is a process, full of ordeals, growth and satisfaction was a new awareness.

"Live and Let Live" is letting others live their lives. It is challenging and means being accountable. This means that they have their own Higher Power in their lives and it is not me. This allows me to focus on myself. It gives me the opportunity to enjoy each day and not interfere with someone else's life.

Through this tolerance, I find humility, faith and self-aware-ness. This became a strong foundation for personal confidence becoming the basis of my life. When I had a life, I was learning to no longer be concerned for the choices, opinions and actions of others. I was free to rally my own needs, and accordingly, my loved ones could live more freely to meet their own needs.

In addition, it means the past is no longer my focus. I do not react from past harms, but can live in the moment, free to be myself. I am able to move forward from this stance and detach from the past with love and forgiveness. This is the moment I have to enjoy life. As I move forward in my progress, my future grows into better places daily.

This new basis in my life has brought rewards I could not have envisioned before. Today I am in a relationship of unconditional love in spiritual unity. My boyfriend has his life of volunteering, bicycling, baseball and bowling that truly make him happy. I am not a part of these activities unless I am invited to a celebration dinner.

I have my counseling, writing, art work, and volunteering for my focus. We both enjoy plays, traveling, golfing and other activities, including our spiritual study group called "Search for God." Our lives are full with each other and filled when we are not with each other.

Before my life changes, I was most devastated because my son would not communicate. I had very teary times during several Mother's Days. He wishes to not participate in many family gatherings either. I learned that I do not have to have my son there for me to be happy. However, I have had to learn he is living his life that works for him.

In the past, my daughter and I were at arm's length in our relationship. Lately, I have become a sounding board for her to make her own decisions. Currently, she calls to check in and sometimes looks to me for "wisdom" when she calls. Nowadays, she calls me often and has learned to depend upon me for loving support. In her last call, I did make several suggestions of options for her to take. She called back, happy with the results that are working out very well for her. She found her own way to resolve her dilemma.

"One good turn deserves another" and that is true inasmuch that what you do to others — or for others — comes around in the course of time and you can, in fact, carry karma from one life to another. Good karma is something that you can gain at any time and particularly where it has involved someone unknown to you.

The big prize through this transformation is that I have developed real feelings. It is safe to express myself, be myself, and feel my feelings. I can now live more fully and I can now allow others to live more fully, too.

Life's Lessons

Creating a universe of lessons
only I can resolve. Looking
outside myself was futile
It only kept the battles brutal.

With courage to look within, I vowed
To fashion a new universe of love.
Releasing every destructive thought, action
Renovating every fragment into compassion.

Through careful searching over years,
valleys and mountains gradually smoothed.
Never-ending, it seemed eternal, wanting
a final test to complete my desire,

A glimmer of truth emerges, finally time for
freedom from struggle. Growing into awareness
of releasing my parental guidance, allocates
God's loving control.

The Secret for Reality

The idea of "One Day at a Time" was new to me. I always had to protect myself from past harms and was very focused on how to be safe. I did not know that I was reliving the past repeatedly and reacting to those old situations. As I worked through the principles presented in my first stories, I was able to leave my history behind, one fear at a time. In addition, I could release my resentments as I was no longer the little five-year-old throwing a temper tantrum that life did not go my way.

As I let go of my past negative thoughts and actions that had been recreating my going around on the hamster wheel, I could now move off the old rotation and into the present time. This frees me not to carry the burdens of the earlier experiences. My head can clear of those messages that kept me reacting as if I was still in the old predicaments.

The emotional damages from punishment were severely ingrained for not getting the chores done as directed. I was beaten, humiliated and shamed for not measuring up to my stepfather's standards and requirements. Therefore, I acted in extremes to be perfect to escape his chastisement. However, there was always another predicament and price to pay. This kept me a victim and always vigilant, trying to stay safe. It felt like I was always in a war zone. Focusing on the past for me was about survival.

At the same time, I had a huge worry about the future, especially my financial security. My fear of not having money began at the age of three. My mother and real father fought every night, and I felt abandoned and without any security in my life. How would I get money for food? If they were not there for me, how would I eat? This fear followed me throughout my life until recently.

My mother was raised during *The Great Depression* in the United States. She taught me well the fear of financial insecurity. I was to keep my meager amount of money from birthday gifts in the bank until a rainy day. I kept track of every penny I had or spent. That was the rule. I never had an allowance to blow on myself. If I did not buy a souvenir on a vacation, that was considered a good choice. Even in my marriage, I wrote down every penny spent for the family. To spend money on me meant I might not have the food I would need in my future.

Therefore, coming to terms that they were sick people and I do not have to follow their demands anymore became freeing. It became essential to release the past and the future, so I could live in the NOW — One Day at a Time.

In my earlier years, I was never in reality, accepting that the past cannot be redone, improved or changed. I can replace the old messages and fire those voices in my head. However, I can make my own rules and give myself approval for my actions. This meant moving beyond my childish endurance. I cannot pray for a better past. It is over.

The past was a fantasy that no longer existed. My worries about the future were unrealistic hope or figments of my imagination. I so much wanted to have everyone get along and treat me decently. My prayers for a happy family were not going to happen. That daydream never came true. I have to create my happiness and not depend on them to make me happy or provide my needs.

Living in the present time is a novel idea. Reality is in the moment to moment. Life is only right now. I have a roof over my head, food for the next meal, a car to get me to my activities. How

I handle my life right now builds my future. If I offer loving help, listen to someone, or do a kindness for someone, it will come back to me. When I drive a friend to the grocery store or contribute my time or money to a good cause, I am creating my potential.

As an adult, I see where I can contribute to others. Instead of a love taker, I become a love giver. My future becomes caring, kindness, and being helpful. I build my own future by how I respond in love now. What I give away returns as abundance.

Now it is possible to make good choices. I no longer react from the past and am acting in loving ways. I make amends where it is appropriate to right my side of the street and trust the universe to give me direction and guidance for my life. The Ego is no longer running my show, I am.

I just do the next right indicated thing as I move through the day. This is the secret for being in reality. Now I can be fully engaged in what is happening around me: the sights, smells, sounds, the people, things, and the ideas that occur. When I learn to value each day, using it wisely and fully, I need not react when it ebbs into yesterdays, nor waste it by projecting my thoughts into tomorrows.

Living one day at a time allows me to brush away my previous days, to let go of my dread of tomorrow, and get on with my life, now. I seize today, put it in order, and fully make it my own. I take time to stop and smell the roses, and take my life One Day at a Time. I am happy in reality. I share my experience and strength, hoping it will enrich your life.

Today I Will:
1. Slow down
2. Enjoy the flowers

3. Be kind to others and myself
4. Remember everything is OK
5. Reduce my expectations
6. Increase my laughter
7. Be less sensitive
8. Hug my lover
9. Not overreact
10. Meet all events with confidence
11. Release the past
12. Enjoy the quality of life's journey

One Bite at a Time—Keep It Simple

I had no idea how to keep my life simple. If you had my responsibilities, problems, and family, you would have a jungle to sort through, too. I had to keep everything afloat in my marriage.

I seemed to be the one responsible for all the errands and projects in the family. I kept everything shipshape in the house with the bills paid and ironing done. My daughter and I cleaned the house every Saturday from the ceiling to the floors. If you visited me, you knew I was a good person because we had a clean house. I fed the family, dressed the children, took them to their music lessons and other activities. I taught all week, worked off hours in our printing business, and did the yard work on Sundays.

I was familiar to crisis, chaos and turmoil. There was always more to do in a day than I could complete. My jobs, my children and husband took priority. There was no time to get my projects done or for myself. With my mind in a muddle and frantically searching for answers, my vision was distorted and preoccupied.

My focus was on everything around me to keep me out of the real focal point that needed to be addressed and resolved. Concerns of "what if" and magnifying the issues took away my clarity. There were so many distractions that when I tried to move through them, they kept me from actually reaching what was needed to be resolved.

As my family grew up and left home, I still had to teach daily, and in every minute not teaching, I was working in our business. Finally, with my divorce and recovery from my many medical issues, learning to reset my attention to myself and not to allow those extraneous diversions get in the way of my progress, made sense.

Self-defeating barriers were stopping my progress. I needed serenity and good orderly direction to proceed. In patience, I can see more clearly the simple steps to achievements and resolutions. A plain, straightforward approach is productive and uncomplicated.

Trying to control the outcome or anticipate everything that can go wrong complicates the issue. It only stresses me out. Reacting from past fearful habits rather than current necessity is not prudent. Feeling paralyzed and overwhelmed makes it more complicated in my mind. Taking more on than I can handle at this moment is unrealistic and overpowering. Needing to see things as they really are, at face value, removes all the fifty things that might or might not follow.

Approaching a project step-by-step keeps it simple. Putting the steps into manageable stages rather than all at once is a handy way to reduce the complexity. Learning the story of "How do you eat an elephant?" was helpful to me. When I heard "one bite at a time," my frustration reduced and I could determine the next small step. My new understanding was just doing the next right thing. I could relax and be gentler with myself. Surprisingly, I could eventually get where I was going.

This week we are experiencing an extreme heat wave. I do not keep the house full of food because walking through the grocery store is painful with my arthritis. However, I sensed that I should stop and shop as I drove by the store early in the week. Now I had milk and the other needed items for my cupboard.

Then I was informed that my friend needed help because of

the extensive heat wave. I phoned her and immediately knew I had to get her out of her overly hot house or she would not make it. She is elderly and not in good health. I picked her up and then needed to fix meals while she was here. Luckily, I had food.

Because my knees hurt from standing to cook meals, I eat what is easy. What could I feed company? I realized I had enough soup from earlier in the week. What could I put with it? I had picked up salad makings and I could handle standing to put that together if I did not have other cooking. I had thawed strawberries the day before. If I made biscuits to bake while I made the salad, we could have strawberry shortcake.

This could be a simple meal instead of a full meal of meat, potatoes, vegetables, salad, etc., without my being in too much pain. She loved the soup make from corned beef broth, meat, and beans. The green salad was refreshing in the hot weather. The dessert was a nice touch. A simple meal did the trick.

The biggest project I ever tackled was writing, *Paradigm Busters, Reveal the Real You.* How do you write a volume that is 600 pages? I was told about halfway through the project by a naysayer, I would never finish it.

Well, thank goodness, I had an editor that set me down and we proceeded to put the chapters in order along with the extra pages of prologue, introduction, etc. Sorting out where the pieces fit became a puzzle. Then, we had to do that within each chapter. Would the 600 pages ever be printed for people to have the information?

I started to put it together one chapter at a time within the framework we had designed. The fact that each sentence had to be in a sequence and make sense within the chapter was hair pulling. However, with her calm approach to rewrite sentences for clarity, gradually it came together, line by line. It had become a sentence-by-sentence project. For two years, I was not able to work on the book; I needed a break.

Then I got a second wind. After 25 years of this process, the book was completed. It did get to press and printed. What a process to keep simple. However, it did work. Now the book is available on Amazon. I am so proud that I did not give up in the middle of the process. It is the ultimate book for personal and spiritual growth. It has stories, tools, and more help.

Keeping it simple for small or big ventures works for me today. It makes life better without the being overwhelmed, trying to do it all at once and determining the outcome. I am eating the elephant more often today, one bite at a time.

'Easy Does It' — Changing Me

Being raised that I have no value, unless I am busy, has been a hard lesson to change. Lying on the grass in the backyard as a child, I was looking up at the billowy cloud shapes in the clear blue sky and enjoying the warm summer breeze, while lying on the comfy green grass. My mom called from the window, "If you do not have anything to do, come in here and I will give you something to do." After that, I always had a job that was necessary for me to accomplish. Punishment awaited me for jobs not done on time or not completed a day earlier than I was told by my stepdad.

I was not familiar with the slogan, "Easy Does It." This saying was foreign to me. Currently, I am trying to recover from being a workaholic and overachiever. In fact, I wonder how I could have taken it easy with my life. My parents always had me doing the chores before I could play. However, the chores were never done, so by afternoon, when I was supposed to go off with the neighborhood kids, I was still working. I thought if I did all these chores, they would think I am a worthy person, and if I were productive, I have value.

What I learned was not to have fun or feel comfortable having fun if the work was not completed. In my life, I always had specific items of what had to be done. This actually helped me in completing my schoolwork. My friends went swimming on the hot days while I stayed home and did my household tasks, homework, or studied for a test. By college the good part of this is that I graduated and they did not.

However, in my marriage I found it hard to go to bed

before the long list was completed. I would go into anxiety. Therefore, I would finish the projects so I could sleep. This meant less sleep on many nights. My jobs never ended.

I applied my workaholic manner in my school teaching. I always had papers to correct, curriculum to write, or to do grades for report cards. Then I could accomplish family things, which was another extensive "to do list" for the evening. A time to relax and enjoy life never seemed to happen.

My husband decided to earn a living with a print shop. Starting up a family business meant long hours into the middle of the night, in addition to my regular routine. During the summers of not teaching, that meant I had to get up and go back to work by eight in the morning, along with cooking all the meals for our family while at the shop. This made a long day. My children were getting a similar routine as I had growing up. It was all work.

For me it was either work at school, at our print shop, or at home. I never had a moment to myself. The pressure was always on. Then one Sunday after church, I was so tired that I wanted to take a nap; I was suffering from exhaustion. I lay down to sleep. My husband came in and picked me up. He carried me outside and said, "If I am working in the yard, you are too."

Finally, I ended up at a psychiatrist's office for help. I was not up to the overachieving and abundance of tasks anymore. He realized I needed a break. I was worn out, exhausted and fatigued. The doctor told me to take two years off from teaching; I needed to do nothing but rest. I was so fatigued that I lay in bed and asked God, "What am I supposed to be doing?" The answer came back that "Now that you are down flat on your back, you are going to learn to meditate." This surprised me, as I did not know how to meditate. That day was the beginning of a new way to handle my life.

However, my workaholic and overachieving is not easy to change for me. I still can get into that mode. If I have a moment, I go to the computer to write, pick up a brush to paint a commission, or meet with a client for counseling. I always have something I can do. This has been harder than quitting any other compulsions I have had.

My parents told me what to do. My husband told me what to do. My job told me what to do. Now in meditation, I receive guidance and follow that. The silent voice offers direction that is most helpful. I am learning to make my own choices. Recently in meditation, I was told I was to take a vacation that means not working and take time for fun activities. Gradually, I have been slowing down and pacing myself more. I have even had a day lately where I did nothing at all.

First Things First

I was always trying to complete my long lists of "to do's." I was overwhelmed, I was so frustrated, and my life seemed unmanageable. My lists always had more to do than I could handle, and my fear was some kind of punishment if the chore was not done, which came from my childhood.

This made a very desperate life in my mind. It seemed to be so overwhelming and I had no clue how to sort it out in my younger days. I was a walking zombie, feeling overpowered and devastated. The shame of this goaded my life. I felt like a juggler in the circus, keeping all the plates on sticks turning, so they did not fall.

There was no way I could resolve them all at once. I was so responsible; I tried, but I was not equipped to cope, and was confused. This all brought on a loss of proportion and distorted my objectives. My lack of order was not productive. I was so intense about the outcome, before I ever got to working out a plan.

I spread myself too thin, trying to do it all at once. I lost sight of the bigger picture. Then I became so frustrated, I had no direction. I have not been a person to give up, procrastinate, or deny the tasks to be done. This was not my way. I was always reminded of what needed to be done. I did lose my sense of proportion, which distorted my objectives.

Recently, I went into this mode of too much to do, and it all had to be done right now. I was beside myself without a way to sort it out. I called my friend, who suggested that I write them all on paper so I could prioritize them. She helped me calm down. Surprisingly, as I picked out the most important project to be first, all the rest of the supposedly drastic items that had to be done were not so severe. Just sorting them out and bringing them into a proper portion to be done seemed to smooth the waters more quickly than in the past. When I tackled the first item, the rest of them seemed almost to take care of themselves. They were no longer large and looming obstacles. I saw how I had created them into much larger tasks.

Learning to use the saying, "First Things First" has reduced the stress and anxiety in my life. It has given me direction and a plan. It helps me remember to consider the importance of my various issues, and to deal with them in their appropriate order. I find that thinking and acting in a logical sequence not only results in efficient solutions and strategies, but it also provides me with a sense of accomplishment and progress. This has strengthened my sense of self. It reassures me that my crises and commitments can all be handled, each in its own time.

Looking back, I think that my Bipolar Disorder kept me in that overwhelming place. Now that I've healed it, I can more easily find good orderly direction. In my old life I overreacted. My recovery has brought me into not reacting excessively. This brings things into a new realistic, more rational perception.

To help me currently move through my list, I find the next right thing that I need to address and focus on just that. This brings me into the Now. Keeping my focal point on what I am doing right now has helped me lose the sense of being over-whelmed.

I pick from my list what are the priority items to tackle. I work on them and move on to the next right thing from my list that needs to be addressed. This actually puts me into a plan that smooths out my mind, and I accomplish the work successfully.

This coming week, my boyfriend is having surgery for his

eyes, so all my lists will be on the back burner until I am free to get back to work. Later this month, we are going to the ocean for some fun. During the trip, my focus will be on enjoying my little vacation. My lists are not my only life. When I return, I am fresh again to revisit the list for the next right item to accomplish.

More work seems to be completed as I move through this scheme. I actually achieve more than I thought was possible for a day, when I had no order to my madness. Now my next challenge is not to get distracted from the plan. I am a curious person and can find myself searching out something on the Internet while on my task. Therefore, that is my next step; to stay on First Things First.

However, First Things First has brought better organization to my work. I get less frustrated about all my many items on the list. I have a list for household errands and shopping, a list for writing, a list of activities with my boyfriend, a list of family and friends with which I need to connect. My clients for the week go on another list. I have many lists. If I stay with the First Things First, it works.

Think

As those of you following my writing each month know, my life was about survival. I reacted quickly to try to stay safe, if possible. I wanted to be included and liked. Even so, I found myself in places that were injurious situations, not only emotionally, but also physically. It had not occurred to me until I decided to change myself for a better life that I was not thinking or acting rationally. My life growing up and in my marriage was dictated to me. Even the dogma in my church told me how to think. I had not learned to think for myself.

My mother intended for me to teach. I received excellent evaluations while teaching in the public schools. She took me to church, where I later taught Vacation Bible classes and sang in the choir. Again, my mother's plans changed me from playing piano to playing flute. Her reason was that I could not march in the band if I played a piano. I could be in the band if I played the flute. My husband had me working in our new business besides my teaching, as we could not afford a bookkeeper. He had me tutored to do the books and tax forms. I did not have to think, they thought for me. On the surface, I looked good to everyone.

I had to change to have my own life; I needed living skills. I had to start thinking for myself. I had to make my own decisions when I divorced. Gradually, I learned to put my intelligence and objectivity before my emotions, willfulness, or passiveness, while considering the consequences for each of my actions. Learning to take responsibility for behavior and myself was a scary step. All these years, I had pushed the decisions onto my spouse.

Daily I took an inventory of my activities and thinking, to see where I still needed to change to apply my new principles and honesty into my present lifestyle. I consciously reframed my attitudes by changing my negative or fearful ones into positive ones. Meditation became a new behavior that seemed to help me find direction and guidance through my new path. In meditation, it distanced me, bringing emotional calmness. I could see the bigger picture and my part in it. Learning to think before I act was a complete turnaround.

I was finding new solutions by thinking. My relatives had a party while I was visiting in another town. The social gathering had been planned before I came to see them. Of course, I was included. I looked forward to meeting their friends. The drinks were poured into the largest glasses I had ever seen, but I do not drink. I started a conversation with a woman and she walked away to the kitchen to be with my relative. I was left all alone at the outdoor umbrella table. The men were off talking, and so I joined the women in the kitchen. I went inside to join everyone there. Again, I tried to be friendly. It seemed that I was not being included in their conversation in the kitchen either. Again, I was left alone as the others left the room, not saying anything to me. This time they went to a small room, where there was no space for me. I took it personally. I felt rejected. Twice was enough.

I decided that if they were not being sociable, I would go to the apartment in the basement, where I was staying, and read my new book. I could make my own entertainment and happiness. I did not need them to entertain me for the evening. I was enjoying myself when I heard the front door close upstairs as they all left. I sat in a recliner, happy with myself and enjoying my special book. I did not have to be liked by them to like me and have a pleasant evening.

Another time was Christmas, when I was enjoying the holiday season with my boyfriend at his home. We had a pleasant Christmas Eve at his church. We came home, where he proceeded to write out large checks as gifts to his children for the next day of festivities and gift giving. We watched some television and then decided to get to bed. I lay there, fuming for some time. I got up and sat in the living room in an inner tizzy. I was not able to sleep in this frenzy. I went into the bathroom and got angry looking in the mirror. I realized from where the anger came. I had to earn every penny I had. Learning to think below the present situation and from where my fury came brought an interesting answer.

I was angry that he gave his children big checks, and I knew I would not get one. No one in my family had ever given me money or a large check for a gift; I was jealous. It brought up the feelings of never receiving money from my parents, yet my half sister got money all the time. I was always left out when it came to a gift of money.

I examined my past year with him and put together all the things he did for me or with me, financially. Realizing that I received more in our activities, trips and events attended, set my anger free. I had gratitude that he was with me and a check would not replace his companionship or the time we shared. The money was not the issue. I was not a victim, but really the victor.

I recognized that the real problem was not the current circumstances, but a repeat of emotions from my growing up and prior events. My sister got money when she asked my parents to help her. After my divorce, I had gone to my stepfather for a loan and was turned down bluntly. I was not given any financial support from my mom or stepdad. His motto was, "We do not spoil Marilyn."

As I was learning healthy tools, I could handle myself more appropriately. I apologized for my anger and settled down. My boyfriend had me go back to bed instead of sleeping in the recliner. It was no longer a problem for me. This allowed me to develop a positive attitude for Christmas Day and achieve serenity as the checks were dispersed with the gifts.

For me, it was about clarifying my mind instead of analyzing, examining and reconstructing. I had to change my emotions and realize that they came from prior situations, and the buttons were pushed from the past. My anger had nothing to do with the present circumstances. The present moment may not always be serene, but I can achieve serenity by allowing each moment to evolve into a positive solution in reality.

This Too Shall Pass

My life was terrible, horrible, and awful growing up. I was sure it would be that way throughout my whole life. It seemed like my life was stuck in cement and would never get better. Even in my older years, it felt like I was doomed to a life of misery. I was always tired, worn out, and busy. It seemed forever. Nothing passed in my life into better times.

When I first heard this saying, I thought it was a joke. This was not possible, so I discounted the message. It has taken years to clean out the past emotional baggage so my feelings do pass and the new good feelings can replace the old ones.

When I began to address my old fearful past to release it, it took about six months before I felt a difference for the first time. I woke up one spring morning to the sun shining and the birds outside were singing. It felt good that morning. What a treat when you never felt good in the morning before going to work or any place. I realized that my old feelings had passed and the good ones had come in. I decided to enjoy the good weather and walk to work. It was a mile walk, but it was such a nice morning, I wanted to take pleasure in it.

This gave me the understanding that the old negativity in my life can leave and I can have a new experience that is high quality. Therefore, I continued to clean out my inner house of remaining old disturbing baggage. I found that if I ask to remove it in prayer that is an altered state of mind, then I can replace it with love and grace. Gradually, my days had good moments. Some days were better as time progressed. I felt better about my life and myself.

I had no idea what grace really was at the time, but I knew it was better than what I had in the past. While camping at Death Valley National Park, I was meditating. What a wonderful site because the energy is so old. Without any warning, I felt grace from head to toe for the first time. It was wonderful.

How do you explain something invisible? It seemed like white billowy clouds inside that were soft, comfy without any harshness. I was emotionally surrounded in this yielding, cozy and relaxing space. Wow! This was new to me. Then, continuing to remove any old harshness and negativity was not a concern. I knew how good it could feel to be in unconditional love.

This experience expanded with more meditation. I found this space of grace when I meditate daily. This feeling began to grow into more and more of my experience. Meditation felt so good with the feelings of grace, I did not want to miss my morning or evening meditations. Later, I often stop in the afternoon, calling it my meditation break instead of taking a coffee break. I like this stress-free place experience. When I return to work, I am refreshed to move forward.

I return to this space more easily and quickly lately. I like having my life in a pressure-free zone. My life is now in more grace than the nervousness of the past. I understand that when I am in grace today, I have moved into a higher consciousness out of the past third dimension of prior fears and harms.

This is my goal in life, to move back into the presence of God. This is a higher quality of life, where there is only unconditional love. I am moving up into a new reality of unconditional love, which is the grace of God.

When I was sick as a child, I was put in a room and told I could come out when I was well. I had no idea of how to help a person when they needed help from medical conditions. In the past, if someone was sick, I went the other way, as I was clueless of what to do. When my boyfriend recently had a stroke and then eye surgery, I could step up to the plate each time and be of assistance easily with a sense of what he needed. I had matured from that sick, scared little three-year-old.

This simply means I have ascended beyond the ego's fear running my life, where I react irrationally and I am in an insane state of mind. In third dimension, my ego is the motivation for survival. In grace, I am immersed in the unconditional love of God without any interferences to stop grace from providing for my needs. *Seek ye first the kingdom of God and all things will be added.* The spirit can manifest my needs and provide for me when there are no barriers for this to happen.

This is how the fish multiplied in the Bible. Grace supplied the needed food for the crowd. A person living in grace will find their needs are taken care of. I am finally able to get a new furnace for my hot tub. For years I have had to turn on the power each time to use it, and that takes more power. It is also inconvenient to wait for the water to heat.

My pool had stopped heating, and I needed a service person to fix this. While he was here doing that, I found out he fixed the leak, too. I had been adding water for several years, not knowing where to find the leak. Then in our conversation, he knew about the kind of heater I wanted. None of my other service people said it was possible to have a heater like I described. My friend has one like this, but every time I tried to find a person to install one, I was told it was not possible with my hot tub. Surprisingly, the date is set to get the new pool heater. It came together easily when I called to get the pool heating again.

When I think back of how my life was thirty-two years ago, in the crisis, chaos and turmoil of fear, I know that the past has moved out of my life. Life is no longer fearful or destructive. No longer do I play the victim and need a person to save or take care of me. I have a relationship of unconditional love with the freedom to be myself, today. I handle life intuitively and find instinctively how to handle new situations. The past is no longer the basis of my motivation to react. I now respond in loving resolutions. Love never fails.

Let It Begin with Me

What I am is what I project to those around me. It took several years to realize that even when I thought I was helpful or caring for others, it was not true. I had nothing to give. I wanted to be a loving mother, a great wife, and terrific teacher. I was a terrific teacher with the subject matter, but my emotional life was in shambles. My students learned the subjects well. However, I was not emotionally available. Gradually, I realized I was not emotionally available to my children or husband. I was sending out my defenses to keep myself safe. It was survival. I was emotionally and spiritually bankrupt inside.

I looked for my stability, love, and saving me outside myself. I thought this would provide my wellbeing. I thought they were to supply my needs. Ultimately, they failed to satisfy my needs and I did not know how to meet my needs either. Thinking others were responsible for my unhappiness by falling short of their being able to be there for me was my focus. I blamed them for my problems. I could not see that the people I picked were not there for themselves. However, I kept my unrealistic ideas that they were responsible for making me happy.

The slogan "Let It Begin with Me" altered my life in a very real way. For years, I thought if people liked my husband, they would like me. This had to change. Living my identity through my daughter and son had to stop. I had to put the spotlight on myself. When I first heard this, I could not believe that I should focus on myself and ask myself what I want. I was taught this is selfish. I knew what my husband demanded, what my children needed, and how to meet the routines for teaching. I had to know all this to be safe and out of the line of attack.

This was a lifelong, embedded trait I had to address. As my children and husband left, I was without an identity. In meditation, I heard that I had to develop a realistic self-esteem and complete myself. I could not blame others anymore for my unhappiness. They did not do it to me; I did it to myself, I found out as I began taking an inventory of my life and applying spiritual principles to my life. This meant I had to get honest with myself. The more self-honesty, the better my results, I discovered.

Taking simple steps to find myself was the best path. I bought a new shower curtain to replace the one I did not like, but was always too afraid to say anything in the past. I picked out one to match my color scheme and I loved the design. This brought a sense of self-esteem for the first time. I was on track to fill myself with what I wanted and who I am. That gave me courage to redecorate the whole house. I loved picking out the white couches and light rugs to replace the dark, dreary colors that had been the theme. In addition, I took a position teaching metaphysics in a junior college when I retired from public school teaching. I was growing into being true to myself. This fit me well as the new me was emerging.

After a trip to Australia and snorkeling at the Great Barrier Reef, I began painting the underwater coral and sea life. This led me to sign up for art lessons, and my art career was ignited from my childhood. I wrote a poem about Sidney, Australia, and other experiences in Australia. This propelled my poetry that was included in my first book.

During a poetry convention in New York, where I went to receive a poetry award, I heard about a writing conference in Santa Barbara, California. There my writing beyond poetry flowered. I attended for seven or eight years while also attending writing classes nearby my home. My first book, *Roses Have Thorns,* was for sale at their conference. I have been writing and illustrating books ever since.

I joined a spiritual study group called *Search for God.* I was asked to give spiritual programs for them, give readings, and I did past life therapy to members and others. I went for new training as a spiritual counselor, psychic and medium, to also give readings and talk to those who have passed over. I became an international board-certified regressionist and certified hypnotherapist to do past life regressions. I traveled around the world to spiritual sites with the Edgar Cayce's A.R.E. In meditation, I was told that this was part of my maturing.

With my new growth in finding myself, I found my lifelong partner in this spiritual study group. My boyfriend and I attended classes for healing through mediumship. He does Pranic Healing and I channel St. John from the Bible for spiritual/emotional information to heal the situation or condition. For many years, we have been available for free weekly healings.

My lessons to be what I wanted in a relationship were new to me. This was a scary step for me. Since he was not a hugger at the time, I had to set the example by hugging. Then I began sharing my feelings when I realized it was safe to do this. At first, he only said, "Where do you want to go for dinner, or what movie do you want to see?" One night, he ran up the stairs from his hot tub, eager to share with me his answer in meditation. Since then, we have been able to share everything we need to about ourselves and have great communication while trusting each other to be open and honest. My being the example was coming back to me.

The universe has spiritual laws. They are laws of transformation. The most simple of the laws is "Love Transforms." It means that no matter what kind of a condition, situation and relationship you are dealing with, when you bring love to that circumstance of life, it will change, it will be lifted, and it will be transformed.

Everything in the earth is ruled by law. We are included in that "everything," for the universal laws are operating in every experience of our lives, no matter who we are or where we are or what we are doing. The essence and purpose of all universal laws and the reason for their existence is to manifest the infinite love of the Universe to you and to me. When I learned to live with universal laws, I changed and my life changed. I created a new reality around me.

When I apply them to my life, they return wonderful results. I am able to send out loving energy to others and it returns. As I gained in self-esteem, self-respect, caring, thoughtfulness, kindness, compassion and nurturing, I project it out to others. What I give away is what I have. It returns in loving appropriate ways.

My life today is nothing like it was as I grew up, or in my marriage of thirty years, or even on my own for fifteen years. It is a life of harmony, joy and feeling successful within. I have feelings, can trust trustworthy people, and am emotionally available. Today, I know who I am and I am proud of it.

St. Francis of Assisi Prayer

Lord, make me a channel of thy peace – that where there is hatred, I may bring love – that where there is wrong, I may bring the spirit of forgiveness – that where there is discord, I may bring harmony – that where there is error, I may bring truth – that where there is doubt, I may bring faith – that where there is despair, I may bring hope – that where there are shadows, I may bring light – that where there is sadness, I may bring joy. Lord, grant that I may seek rather to comfort than to be comforted – to understand, than to be understood – to love, than to be loved. For it is by self-forgetting that one finds. It is by forgiving that one is forgiven. It is by dying that one awakens to Eternal Life, Amen

Interestingly, that I am writing this part of the book on Francis's Feast Day, October 4, is unintentional. As I was quickly looking for anything interesting to include in my piece, I found that this day is significant in certain religious groups. I am thrilled to be able to share how much this prayer has helped me on this day of celebrating St. Francis, who now has reincarnated as the current pope.

I first read this prayer as an adult from a book that alcoholics use. In my childhood, all prayers came from a hymnal. Therefore, finding this written prayer was great. The first time I read it, I did not understand how deep and meaningful this prayer is. When I was still new in trying to understand its many parts, I had a difficult evening. I wanted to go to a support group meeting to find some answers for my life. I thought it would help me find the answers to my problem. My husband would not agree to drive to the spiritual meeting. We had been driving home and we were going by the place where the meeting was being held. I was most upset over not being understood in my life. In fact, I was fuming.

When we arrived home, I decided to get into the hot tub and say this prayer to myself. I thought this would be helpful. It certainly was. As I remembered different parts of this prayer, the words, *"to understand, than be understood"* came into my mind powerfully.

In a second, I realized that God understood me and that is all that mattered. Others did not have to understand me because God did. That was the best validation and acceptance I could have. Immediately my mind changed into a better attitude. I understand now that I moved from being needy to finding I was not needy; God was there for me. That is all that mattered. He understood me. This brought a new light into my life. I had always felt needy and now it was gone. I was understood. God was supplying what I required. A new security came into my life that has become the bedrock of my being today.

As I go through each section of the prayer, I find it transforms me from my ego's thinking into a higher consciousness. Let us start with the first phrase, *"Lord, make me a channel of thy peace."* Growing up, I was not allowed to ask for things. I had to accept what was given me, good or bad. So asking for peace was a foreign idea. How could I be a channel of God's peace? My life was unmanageable and chaotic in domestic violence. That was a dilemma in those days. I wanted peace, but I did not know how to achieve this.

The next part is *"that where there is hatred, I may bring love."* I did not think that I hated, but I sure was not happy with my life and the people in it. I definitely disliked my situation, but my vocabulary for key words was missing. I did not use the word hate, but in reality that would be a good word for how I felt back then.

My lack of understanding love came from not having that experience. My father and mother were incapable of loving themselves and therefore I was not loved either. This was a major lack in my life, besides not having a stable home in which to grow. There was hatred and no love for years. Thank God, today that has reversed.

"That where there is wrong, I may bring the spirit of forgiveness," was the first time I even read the word forgiveness. No one in my family ever had the spirit of forgiveness. My husband remembered it all and never forgave, just like my family. This word is crucial in my life today. This frees me to be myself. I am happy to forgive.

Forgive means to "give" up the past "for" a new day. I do not have to carry the emotional pains of the past anymore. I can release them like cutting the chains to that emotional connection. I can be free of that attachment which spoils today. I am free of the abuse and harms to live a life in the moment.

The phrase, *"That where there is discord, I may bring harmony,"* adds so much to my life today. Instead of creating more crisis and turmoil, I can provide truth and agreement. I was so used to chaos that I stirred it up to have that familiar feeling. I like not keeping my life in turmoil. I have learned how not to contribute to the discord. I do not have to do that today. It is not comfortable anymore to live life in a frenzy.

My favorite part is *"that where there is error, I may bring truth."* Since I found the truth, I love to share it. That is what my life is about today. Knowing the truth has set me free of all the craziness and misinformation I endured. I find as I share more truth, it comes back to me in wonderful ways. My life is a channel of peace today.

I did not know about faith growing up or from church. The next phrase is *"that where there is doubt, I may bring faith."* It was not until I turned to spirituality did the understanding of faith emerge and how necessary that is. I did not believe that God was there for me; I was not worthy. Therefore, I did not walk in faith. There was no one I could rely on, and I very carefully tried to set up the results so I would not get hurt one more time. Learning that God was to bring the results brought better consequences than my trying to play God in my life. I gave up my doubts completely and found that total faith brings the best answers to all my concerns.

"That where there is despair, I may bring hope" is one of my favorite parts of the prayer. I had no hope several times in my life. I learned over time, I had a death wish. I thought I was doomed to have a terrible, horrible life. I tried so hard to make my marriage better than my childhood, but it just would not come together. I thought I could make a happy family; however, I unknowingly just reenacted the one from which I came. Today my hope is ultimately that my family will all come into harmony and love.

"That where there are shadows, I may bring light" was a new idea to me. I was not familiar with the concept of moving from the dark into the light. This is the major message of the Bible, but I never heard it in my fifty years of attending church.

After that is the part, *"that where there is sadness, I may bring joy."* Again, this was interesting as in my family there was no joy. How could I bring joy when I had none? Currently, the joy creeps in strongly when I am helping others.

When I read, *"Lord, grant that I may seek rather to comfort than to be comforted"* reversed my looking outside for my answers and help, but rather to be there for someone else. I always looked to people to be there for me, especially my parents. When they were not there, I used others as security. This totally changed my focus from "poor me" to "how can I help you?"

Subsequently, *"to understand, than to be understood"* became a new basis for living. That God always understood me, even if my parents and others did not. I was understood. Next, *"to love, than to be loved"* brought new understanding that I was to be a love giver and not a love receiver. I had all my love from God, and I was to pass it on. That broke the bank right there. I found I was not missing love, I was not aware of all the love God had for me.

"For it is by self-forgetting that one finds" became a new perception that I was to forget about clearing the way for my selfishness and survival, not to stop my seeing the reality of God's love in my life. My focus of a bigger picture of struggles can help someone else as I come through them. I found myself in helping others, from my experience of my coming out the other side.

Then, *"It is by forgiving that one is forgiven."* Learning when I forgive others, I am actually forgiving myself. These people played out the parts of me that needed healing and love, to move back into wholeness. I was forgiving myself for all the tribulations, and they had played the part in forcing me to see I had to forgive them; they were my mirror.

Finally, *"It is by dying that one awakens to Eternal Life."* We die to our human faults so our eternal life can come forward and be known. My selfishness dies as it had covered my true self. I am a Christed being releasing my human faults. I then rise into or awaken into eternal life.

This prayer takes me out of my selfish and egocentric ways of survival to become selfless in serving others in God's love. Like the cream in unpasteurized milk rises to the top, my love comes into my life to be "The New Me" *

* See *Roses Have Thorns,* the poem "The New Me"

Peace At Last

Peace has come to my inner storm
Years of torment, abuse and more.
Daily searching for deep answers to reveal
my soul's moving out of past evil.
Returning to one with God constantly means
inner fears, guilt, shame releasing,
imbedded in my mind,
Peace waits for me to find.

Slowly more comes to light
That controlling with all my might
Continues the anguish and despair,
it's time to find a way to repair.
My old ideas need to change.
Transformed into a loving encompassing range,
healing myself and extending it to others;
even if those harming me are not my brothers.

Forgiveness for all including myself
Creates equality, among ourselves.
Moving toward wholeness through inner love
Brings blessing to all from an inner caring heart.

PART THREE

FINDING HEALTH AND SANITY

The Truth About Alcoholism and Drug Addiction

Who wishes to continue in misery, wretchedness and depression? Alcoholism is an incurable disease that ends at the time of death. However, this interim period between the two points can be extended into a normal, happy and productive life if one accepts and practices the necessity for treatment for the rest of his or her life. Thousands of people today claim a daily healing from this malady, and as a result, enjoy living. With truthful information, no one in this enlightened age has to suffer, however denial is prevalent.

A couple years ago, our country spent $175 million in a campaign from the Office of National Drug Control Policy to perpetuate the myth that if people drink responsibly they would not become alcoholic. This is not accurate. The American Medical Association declared it a disease. There are hereditary, genetic and generational predispositions to becoming an alcoholic.

General McCaffrey stated when he was in office that the "challenge was to reverse the current sharp rise in illegal drug use by youth." The reality is the old adage: monkey see and monkey do. Add elements of inherited and family history to this population that digests alcohol and drugs differently than a regular drinker, and the story becomes more complex. Youth feel emotional pain, fear and anger from household factors, and see the disowning and drowning of their parents' misery. Are emotional wounds, pains and undiagnosed medical problems some reasons for youth acting out in violence?

Alcoholism, drugs (including prescriptions), cigarettes, work, sex, and other addictions such as co-dependency, violence and abuse anesthetize and hide the anguish about which no one talks. The kids turn to substitutes for escape and self medication from their family lineage. When an adolescent smokes pot, it is the same as the adults smoking cigarettes. They are doing the same activity — covering their feelings; however, one is more acceptable by our culture. Both experience the same dilemma.

Programs that encourage saying "NO" are uninformed that it is a health condition. The first time of indulging may relieve the pain of this disorder. As the "progression" of the disease grows, relief is what the user wants. Physiological imbalances in a body do not listen to reason. It is like saying "no" to cancer. The "war on drugs" will not stop the problem.

Reducing the demand occurs when the addicted person is in remission with a daily program reinforcing the honesty that they are bodily and mentally different from other people. Their body chemistry does not digest alcohol or drugs like typical drinkers. Therefore, when the person reaches the point of healing, the desire for mood-altering substances will not be as strong as the desire to live a healthy life. This is called healing or recovery.

The American Medical Association declared addiction a chronic, progressive disease that leads to death or insanity without intervention. There are three stages to this disease:

1. Early Stage

In the early stages, the alcoholic can outdrink his friends. The disease is so subtle that first revisions in the liver and central nervous system increase tolerance and often improve performance. Tolerance or drinking large amounts transition to maintenance drinking. This shift promotes an even level of alcohol in the blood, so the person drinks to function.

2. Middle Stage

Moving into the middle stage is not clearly defined. However, three characteristics are basic features. They are the physical dependence as experienced in acute and protracted withdrawal syndromes, craving, and loss of control. Later stages include withdrawal convulsions, hallucinations, and *delirium tremens* (DT's).

3. Last Stage

The last period kills the person one way or another. Suicides, accidents, drowning, fires from passing out with a lighted cigarette, falling, or car crashes are a few of the unlisted causes of symptoms. It attacks the heart, liver, brain, stomach, lungs, kidneys and pancreas. It even causes cancer. Malnutrition is common.

Basis for Recovery

To recover from a dependency on alcohol and drugs, you need to do three things.

1. *Accept that this is a sickness.* The person has a chemical imbalance similar to diabetes.

2. *Detox.* Find either a local treatment center using a 12-step program or one like the Betty Ford/Hazeldon Treatment Centers and attend Alcoholics Anonymous meetings. These are ways to accept reality.

3. *Add a spiritual program to help a daily pardon.* Changed attitudes can bring happiness and healthiness. Many people don't view health as an exciting path, until they don't have it.

Communities now are preoccupied with drug abuse in teen suicides or recent killings at schools, entertainment events, or malls. Community structure deteriorates as money is drained into programs too narrow for proper intervention and effective results with the primary illness. Retaining the whole perspective is necessary. It is the nature of the disease to take one part and scapegoat the rest. This complex picture cannot embrace short-term, quick fix solutions. Overreacting to a long-term problem fails to assess the total scope of the difficulty. We need to accept and see this malady in its wholeness.

Unfortunately, many in the health field do not understand the effect of the drugs they prescribe. We have come to a time for communities to identify the rage and grief for drug-related suicides and killings from irrational thinking processes.

I wrote a news release about this.

Robert A. Hawkins, 19, opened fire with a rifle at a busy Omaha shopping mall, killing eight people before taking his own life. Looking back, we had the tragedy at Virginia Tech caused by Cho Seung-Hui. And the first of the series of heart-breaking disasters was Columbine in 1999. Sadly, these results of drugged youth are a deadly price to others. That the students were on prescriptions is not widely shared.

The therapists and doctors do not realize that emotional growth and rational thinking stops when taking drugs. Let us support our youth in dealing with their problems utilizing effective, natural drug-free solutions. Antidepressant-induced manic behaviors like fire starting, violence and aberrant behaviors are the result of looking for a quick fix while sustaining high profits for drug companies. Drugs do not help or heal these multifaceted based problems. It is time to support our youth in dealing with their problems with effective, natural drug-free solutions.

We need to refocus our attention on an ongoing assessment process that is all inclusive. A sound planning effort for the entire continuum of adolescents and adults in drug dependence needs implementation and development in physical, mental, emotional and spiritual parts of the person's life. The issue is not a lack of alcohol, drugs, or medications needed in the body, but the difficulty in adjusting to adulthood. Let's do the right thing, not what is politically correct. People are dying. This is not drug abuse; it is ignoring reality. Action means more to the ill than talking about stigmatizing sick people who can transform their lives into becoming a contributing citizen to our society.

Treat Violence as a Disease

Violence is a disease process or can be part of addiction/ alcoholism/drugs. How do you legislate or punish a genetic, hereditary and/or generational disease? Programs that address the root cause and origin of the issues are the only ways to heal violence. People act out their pain and anger; it is a cry for help.

Words to describe violence are endless as aggression, fighting, hostility, violent behavior, brutality, cruelty, sadism, bloodshed, carnage, killing, slaughter, massacre, butchery, and more. The list did not include war, battle, conflict, or combat. Our society is being conditioned into violence through the evening news, which is mostly about violence. Then there are the video games, movies, DVDs, television, and more.

Even in theater, musicals and plays like "Assassins" acclaim this action by celebrating the killings in song and dance. It uses the premise of a murderous carnival game to produce a revue-style portrayal of men and women who attempted to assassinate Presidents of the United States.

Where does the motivation for violence begin, in the home? Some families think sarcasm, mockery, ridicule, scorn or disrespect is okay. Often parents do not know the difference between discipline and punishment. Discipline teaches the child to find a better way to resolve their problem. It is not about physical harm. Habitually, if the parent was beaten, so will his children receive the same treatment.

Raising a child in love and stability is not easy in our lifestyles today. However, it is the only way for a youngster to grow up with a rational and caring life. Parents advise in helping the adolescent make good decisions that are positive, with positive results. They provide for the needs of the child to be met appropriately. They support the adolescent with encouragement and showing/helping them how to do the project.

Instead of punishing a child, which stops their emotional growth and self-esteem, you allow them to find another option that will work better. No one is wrong. When the parent sits down with them and lets them figure out the better way to resolve the problem, they determine another way to handle the issue. The parent is allowing them to take responsibility and validating them for doing it. This provides communication between the two of you and a bonding. This brings a sense of belonging and family.

The parent listens to the requests, thoughts or suggestions. The child is accepted as part of the family. Without trust, communication and feelings, the family is dysfunctional. This results in anger, resentment, guilt, and more negative feelings of unworthiness. After years of a lack of looking to release the painful feelings of not belonging in the family, honesty, acceptance, love, and being included with respect, the child becomes ready to strike out.

They either lash out at themselves or others. If it is themselves, it could be suicidal, cutting themselves, sabotaging their life from opportunities, giving up on themselves, becoming depressed or moving into drugs/alcohol, or mental illness to run away from life.

Some, on the other hand, strike out at others. They want to get rid of their emotional pain and harm others by killing, fighting, or harming another. This, of course, does not stop their pain and it grows. The next time there is more rage to release. They may burn down a home or business. They find more angry youth and together more damage is done to others to pay for their painful past.

Anger Management is a superficial way to avoid the deeper dilemma. The band-aid approach of changing behavior usually focuses on the obvious symptoms, not the deeper problems. The violence is a warning sign of a chronic, progressive, fatal disease. It is in epidemic proportions in our country. With the tragedy at Virginia Tech, Columbine and others, red flags as the Menendez brothers, O.J. Simpson and local cases, what else need occur before people recognize that current solutions are not working? Because the media sensationalizes and does not always provide accurate information, public judgments form without all the data.

Professionals who work in health centers, who have not resolved their own anger problems, only offer a shallow approach which is not permanently effective. I know a man who projected his rage towards his wife. He went to Anger Management and came out with the slogan, "Do not harm others." He was convinced that this would stop his injuring his wife. Ironically, in defending his new stance, he became angry with me for offering a deeper insight for resolution. Fortunately, I was able to stand my ground and observe his anger without taking offense. He got on a chair and was shouting in the restaurant that he would not harm his wife.

I knew his wife and some of their story. When I met her later, she told me that he had attacked her again and she was filing for a divorce. How many stories are told of the people who did not find the Anger Management classes useful? It is protected to preserve the image that if a person takes a class, they can be "fixed."

Let us stop the denial and talk about the elephant in the living room. The violence reported is a warning sign of a far deeper, more complex problem, which includes physical, emotional and mental dysfunction. Realizing that all forms of aggression originate from deep inner problems beyond those identified visually, is the answer.

Violent people are addicted to the natural drug adrenalin. The American Medical Association declared addiction a disease in 1956. These sick people need appropriate treatment. Only with truth, knowledge and compassion can people seek the help they need to restore a rational lifestyle. They are compensating for a chemical imbalance from their life being out of a sense of balance.

When a person's needs are not met, they act out in anger to express this. Anger with inappropriate behavior creates hurting others or themselves, acting out their pain. In addition, if the person is using drugs, prescriptions, medications or alcohol, the anger is compounded from the addition of drugs.

Part of treatment is learning to express their anger appropriately. It has been the lack of the ability to express their feelings and being heard that is the problem. In addition, they need to learn healthy responses to old feelings. Then the individual can grow into maturity with appropriate responses of loving resolutions.

When a person is in dis-ease, it leads to disease without intervention that is genuine. Healing from valid information to find the missing balance in the physical, mental, emotional and spiritual aspects is the answer. Individuals can receive the necessary knowledge and appropriate counseling to change the direction of this descending spiral which leads to tragic consequences. This persistent disease grows more severe over time and ends in insanity or death for themselves or others.

Reality will set them free of their hopelessness, despair and depression. The courage to look within for the truth is usually not encouraged. Few seminars, lectures and consultations reveal the dynamics of violence. My interview and lectures on YouTube have tools and understanding that support recovery. The old myths and nonproductive answers continue to bring misinformation.

I attended a three-day workshop on domestic violence given by the local county. I received a big notebook of charts and old information that provide help to women. When I questioned the leader about the woman needing to take corrective measures to change herself, I was dismissed as it is always the man's fault.

I was not allowed to speak to the community service groups after completing the class. There was no acknowledgement that each person needs to take responsibility for what they are sending out to others. My experience was that I was receiving what I sent out. When I changed, I got back loving experiences and the violence was not an issue.

I had a counseling client who was attending classes at the local hospital for women in domestic violence. She looked at me during one session and said, "You understand, but at the hospital where I have to take the classes, they do not get it." In the newspaper two years later, the hospital articles reported that the women were returning and they could not understand why.

It does not matter if the anger is taken out on a community, school, themselves, or another person, the answer is the same. Resentments are a way of saying the person did not do what I wanted them to do, they did not do it my way, or life is not going the way I want. This is an inadequate adjustment to adulthood.

Therapeutic Hypnosis and Holistic Counseling address the total complex issues for a balanced and whole life. Personal recovery is possible with accurate solutions for healing the root causes. Each person can recovery and move beyond their reacting. Let us show kindness, and provide appropriate healing. It is time to present hope and compassion for those hurting. Recovery means people create their own productive, contributing lifestyle that benefits society.

Domestic Violence Has a Spiritual Answer

Most people watch the news reports and hear about domestic violence from a one-time incident. The focus is usually on the belligerent partner being considered the aggressor, while the passive victim is offered sympathy. Some of these newsworthy events, especially the famous O.J. Simpson trial, observed through the media, focused only on the single fatal event. However, a long history leads to the final newsworthy episode.

My story began as a child raised in domestic violence. My paranoid schizophrenic mother married my alcoholic father during *The Great Depression*. Financial security meant safety from abuse, abandonment and economic concerns. My father had a reliable job. She told me once, "You get married for the man to take care of you." This did not deter the nightly fights I heard instead of a lullaby.

One night when I was three, my bedroom door was left open by mistake.

"I'll teach you a lesson!" My father held my mother and was hitting her with a brush.

"Let me go, leave me alone!" Mom yelled.

"You have to listen to me, do you hear?" The screams continued. "If you don't do as I say, you are going to get hurt!" he shouted.

I wonder why the door is open tonight? I asked myself. *My door is always shut at bedtime.* Then I heard, "You are hurting me."

I hate these fights. I'm too little to save her and too fearful to do anything to help. I was terrified watching my father harm my mother. *How can I save my Mom?* I pulled the sheet over me. *I want to be off the face of the earth,* I prayed. I felt hopeless. I buried this feeling with the helplessness. *I should recue my mother and I should be guilty for hiding.* I became the all-time victim from thinking, *Dad will be in here to hurt me next. I have to become as small as possible so I cannot be seen.* I tightened my muscles and nerves to become smaller and completely crawled under the sheet.

"Who left this door open? Shut it quickly. I don't want her to know about our fights."

But I did know about the every-night fights. Even the neighbors knew! I had become a turtle that night, emotionally, to protect myself. Usually, I stayed inside my shell as protection. This was sort of a blessing when, two years later, I was victimized by my soon-to-be-brother-in-law.

That one night the door to my room was left open, a deep scar remained in my soul. My childish instincts tried to protect me. I tightened my turtle-like shell of protection to shield me from physical harm. In addition, I tightened my muscles like a violin string, as tight as possible, thinking I would be too small to be found to be hurt next in my three-year-old body. It was as if I was still attached to my mother and was battered, too. In addition, I prayed to be off the face of the earth, to be sure I would not be around to endure the physical harm from being attacked like her. It took years to determine that my last prayer was translated in my subconsciousness as a death wish.

The shell of protection kept me stuck emotionally at the age of three for most of my life. The tight muscles became Fibromyalgia over the years of strain on my nerves and muscles trying to protect me from any abuse. In addition, my ballet lessons also enhanced the tightening of my muscles.

My next major impact was mother's remarrying. My stepfather was a rageful man and a sex addict. While I was in high school, his 24/7 attacks emoting emotional incest lasted until his death in old age. He was like a vampire in my life, sucking my emotional energy. This deeply scared my soul, too.

In addition, I brought karma from several past lives of domestic violence with my husband into this lifetime, finally to resolve. This life was to become my opportunity to change my energy and resolve my fearful reactions to responding in love.

Music had become my protection and escape from the abuse and insanity throughout my life. I met my husband in the college music department. We were in many classes together, learning to teach music in the schools. After a session of practicing our instruments, we began conversations in the practice rooms. It seemed that we could talk easily, and he even asked for my opinions at times. Growing up, I was to be seen and not heard, so this seemed wonderful, that someone actually would listen to me. Going for a 10-cent cup of coffee to continue our talks was a real treat to a poor college student in the Fifties.

We became an item during our sophomore and junior years in spite of our breaking up a couple of times because of his anger. By our senior year, we were engaged. I was ready to call it off completely, for the reason that I did not want to be around his raging anymore. I found myself pregnant. In those days, society cruelly judged unwed mothers, and I was filled with shame. However, he became my knight in shining armor by marrying me. I was now socially acceptable.

All went well until he was beginning his first teaching position in a school district where there had not been a music department. He was dedicated to setting up their first department. Six months into our marriage, one Sunday evening in

October, he wanted sex. Exhausted from taking care of a new baby girl, I said, "No." He came after me as I entered the living room, from putting her down for the night. He strangled and raped me. This event was ignored and never brought up to be discussed. I learned never to say "No" again. My battering and abusive marriage of rape lasted thirty years.

The next couple of years went smoothly as we were both teaching and enjoying our family. Arguments over choices for our new home began as we were helping to build it with the contractor. They ranged from the carpet choices to other selections needing to be made to complete our rising dwelling. The light fixtures were a big issue, but the most difficult one emerged regarding the phone.

I saw no reason for a single party line and paying more. I had grown up with an eight-party line, then a four-party line and lastly a double-party line. That was a huge improvement. I liked the idea of the two-party line and not listening to others on the same phone line. I found myself on the kitchen floor with him sitting on me, insisting on a single phone line, beating my head on the floor until I agreed.

Over the years, his evolving temper tantrums, rage and unhappiness were projected onto me and onto our son, who came along later. An unspoken message was that I was responsible for his outbursts. Because I had no self esteem or life skills, I learned to be the victim in these situations. I carried the responsibility for his emotional outbursts. Everything in the family was to make him happy, please him, or to do for him. He manipulated everything, even my paycheck from teaching. It was not safe to speak up.

Over time, our son seemed to bring up his anger. Nothing he did was right as far as my husband thought. Both of our children achieved high scores on intelligence tests. However, because of the family dysfunction, they could never use their potential in school and their lives. This problem keeps being passed on in families until someone chooses not to continue the game being played out.

He tried to kill me several times, and I tried suicide several times to escape from the marriage. My life was unmanageable. It was like walking in a mine field and not knowing when the bombs would go off. Or, I was walking on eggshells, people pleasing, and looking good when teaching and socializing. I related with the actress Carol Channing's comment on Larry King's talk show on television, that her husband stayed with her at parties, so she would not spill the beans.

Today I can identify the family roles in the members of a dysfunctional family play. This has become a big aid in my counseling, speaking, and writing. This clarifies the dynamics of each person's behavior, emotional state, and mental basis for their actions.

What did I learn about domestic violence over a lifetime of abuse and more than thirty years of recovery? First, I learned how to stop the hostilities. One night, he was coming after me in a rage where I saw him breathing smoke like a bull ready to charge. The short story is he cornered me in my son's room with only a single bed between me and my husband. He had jumped over a king size bed to strangle and rape me once. This was no deterrent. I was traumatized.

Time stopped while angels held him as if he was a statue, which stopped his advancing towards me. A silent voice inside told me to pray for him. It suggested, "God forgive him for he knows not what he does." Then I added, "God bless him." I said this twice. Next, I was told to leave the room. I was sure as I passed him, I would certainly be attacked. This brought angels to escort me into the hall, unharmed. I immediately turned around to see what would then happen. I wish I had had a camera. His facial expression was indescribable.

I came to understand that when you send love, there is nothing to attack. I had subconsciously been sending out invisible bullets, trying to protect myself from a subconscious level. He retaliated outwardly to defend himself. When this is continued, it becomes raising the ante like in a poker game. This passive aggressive game is often called "King of the Mountain" by children. At the height of this emotional battle, I stopped the game by sending love, which was praying for him. He never touched me again. Love never fails.

Realizing that my emotional life was like an iceberg because what I did not know about myself was the problem. My trying not to be harmed actually was causing the difficulty of his needing to protect himself on a subconscious level, too.

Part of the time, I was the real issue. I found that what you fear is what you attract; therefore, I found out that my fear to not be physically hurt attracted it back to me. I began to change myself by releasing my fears. My biggest fear was of physical safety. In addition, I also had to release other negative emotions, unconstructive messages, lies, and become as honest with myself as possible.

In addition, I found my mother passed on to me her negative energy of abuse. A key unspoken message from my mother was that it is not safe to be in reality, I realized later. Because of this, I was stopping love, thereby sabotaging myself from what I truly wanted.

By identifying and releasing the negative fear, thoughts, and behaviors individually, I was able to replace those old emotions with love, grace, and later compassion.

The rest of the solution came by addressing my physical, mental, emotional and spiritual life. I found that my physical abuse is an extension of mental and emotional abuse at a soul level. I was co-dependent, propelling my life down the tubes. I needed to forgive myself and outgrow my past hardships to find my own self-esteem.

I realized that my neediness was my problem. I had been trying to fulfill my needs from other people, places and things. Using others to supply my needs was not working. Our society has been taught to look outside of ourselves for love and security, but I have found that nothing outside yourself can save you or give you peace. When we stop looking outside of ourselves, we find the truth of who we are.

I was given the answers to life; it's no longer a mystery. And I like to share the message that all we need to do is direct our energy the right way. The lesson is to shift into sending love to all challenges and that love can return. Everybody can do that if they choose to. You don't have to belong to any organization. It's simply a matter of learning what works in your life and how to rearrange it so it works even better. No one can attack love. Love never fails.

My plan was to replace the fear with love. We are all in one loving spirit. In addition, I stopped putting myself in places to be hurt. Therefore, the restraining order and subsequently my divorce would be my way into a healthy lifestyle. I wanted to live in the love of God. It finally would be safe to have a loving standard of living.

Since I cannot change another, my focus changed from my husband to taking care of myself. The first step to my growth was to address my health issues. Healing my twice broken tailbone began my healthy new life. Then, I found that mentally I had to substitute negative thinking for positive thinking. I could change my life by altering my thoughts and beliefs. I now saw that *all things work for good* ... as in Romans 8:28. Over time, I discovered that beliefs come from my head and I gave up all my beliefs to move into my new heart-based life. Therefore, I would rely on my inner guidance for my answers today. I learned to trust my higher power and myself.

The depth of my past emotional life needed to be released and transformed by forgiveness into higher loving feelings of compassion and gratitude. I found myself feeling compassion for my ex-husband when he died two years ago. In prayer I thanked him for the part he played in my life, so I had to turn to my inner love in my heart. I realized his hard childhood was his projection onto me. He acted out his pain. It was so difficult that I had to pray for help, I did not want to die in the marriage. Because of this experience, I found the God within, instead of a God of the hymnal prayers or an abused husband.

Doing an inner house cleaning of old fears, guilt and shame, I found them to be stumbling blocks and obstacles to what I really wanted. This included discovering my past life karma of three other lives we had prior in domestic violence, which was a deeper basis for my miserable life. However, to let go of them and move beyond into the loving life I had always dreamed took work.

Most people call this process *peeling the onion*. However, I knew from spiritual groups and recovery programs that when the spiritual malady was resolved, my mental and physical problems would fall into place. Therefore, I started a path to list, address and transform every negative one and replace it with love and the grace of God. I became fearless and empowered.

This course of action was changing me. I was becoming a Christed spirit releasing my human faults, instead of a human being having a spiritual experience. I started attracting different people into my life that were more pleasant, kind and caring.

Sorting out spiritual principles from religious dogma created a huge challenge to me. I came from a church that was very traditional and fundamental. In fact, I had been taught not to meditate because the church had all my answers. My first attempts to meditate were fruitless. However, when faced with being in bed from physical and emotional exhaustion, I lay there and asked God, "What am I supposed to be doing?" The silent answer came, "Now that I have you flat on your back, you are going to learn to meditate." I decided to open my heart and whatever God told me, I would listen. I started receiving information to help me heal my relationship with myself and for understanding about my mother and husband.

Then the next year, I was abandoned on a trip out of state by my still husband. I went to the beach for my spiritual answers. I sat on a piece of driftwood, waiting for my answer. The answer was not what I expected; in fact, it scared me to death. I was to ask for a temporary separation. Because I was still emotionally three years old, this was difficult for me.

I found out that besides receiving guidance from the silent voice inside, you have to take action, too. Speaking up to my husband was not safe, and I really did not want to do this. However, when I returned home, praying constantly on the airplane for the courage to say this, I did tell him my request. I know today if I had not acted on that direction, I would not be alive today.

On my own growing beyond my three-year-old emotional space, I found that "Safety is the complete relinquishment of attack." *A Course in Miracles*, T.92. Today, my current relationship of sixteen years is based in mutual respect and unconditional love. I had to grow into the qualities that I wanted in a companionship, spirituality, loyalty, sincerity, honesty and trustworthiness, to attract another person who had these qualities. I was not looking for someone to take care of me. I was looking for an equal partner. In my life today, I am emotionally available, can trust, and communicate in honesty. Today, my sixteen years of unconditional love is pleasant, caring, and kind.

Today, my fellow treats me like a queen.

It's called reality!

I no longer,
need to see the bad more
than the good !

Angelica's Gifts © 1996

Pearls of wisdom for success

- Always do the best you can instead of just getting by
- Help others along the way from your experience
- Give to others in beneficial ways
- Invite people to assist you in your weak areas
- Retain your confidence when rejected
- Make the planet a better place

Bipolar Disorder is Not Forever

The side effects of prescriptions became worse for me than the diagnosed disorder. That was the reason I stopped taking drugs. In fact, I realized that medications were blocking my progress out of Bipolar Disorder. I currently have over sixteen years with no medications and was declared sane by my psychiatrist several years ago.

Healing methods promoting rational thinking and healthy behaviors, in addition to prayer and meditation, provided me with sane thoughts and the normal life I was pursuing. After employing alternative holistic methods that were not toxic to my system, I found that the drugs were creating difficulty to function in a normal manner.

In the past, most people were under the impression that Bipolar Disorder would be a life-long ailment. Often it is destructive to relationships, careers, can wreak havoc on family life, and is a potentially fatal disease. According to Edgar Cayce, the Father of Holistic Health, "There are in truth no incurable conditions." Thank goodness, a diagnosis did not have to be a lifetime sentence.

Research now proves this out. Russian biophysicist and molecular biologist Pjotr Garjajev now has scientifically proven that affirmations, along with meditation and hypnosis (another term for meditation), will raise consciousness, increase well-being, and balance chemistry in individuals, even changing DNA. Bipolar Disorder is no longer a final verdict.

Over time, working with holistic counseling that uses therapeutic hypnosis and other energy raising tools suggested by Pjotr Garjajev, people are finding a new life free of their past debilitating illness. With the help of an appropriate counselor that works with the body, mind, and spirit, change in emotions, attitudes, and a new lifestyle releases the root causes and conditions of this disease.

In addition, I found in releasing and healing my trauma and fear, called Post Traumatic Stress Disorder, I become centered and grounded. I found that PTSD was the catalyst below the Bipolar Disorder.

"With new life skills and a spiritual daily program, the old mood swings and extreme behaviors minimized into reality, after discontinuing medications. Fortunately, my psychiatrist supported being off medications," I shared in an interview. Since medications affect each person differently, this might not be good for everyone. My choice was a personal decision. However, I love my sane life today.

My incident that encouraged stopping my medications came from a friend helping me see how drugged I was after taking a pill. He suggested stopping the prescription so I would not be drugged. The medical profession only looks at the symptoms. I found that there was a way to address the underlying problem and there would be no symptoms to medicate. In effect, when using the prescriptions, I was emotionally running away from reality. The drugs kept me in fear and acting out from past trauma. They even stopped my emotional growth, so I could not move beyond the past to improve my condition.

After the initial honeymoon, the side effects became worse over time than the problems. I was developing Parkinson's like tremors in my hands. My articles and books address moving beyond fear, anger and negative behaviors. They have the steps to become sane. My writing guides the reader through "the process" of being restored to sanity.

From childhood, I lived in the fear that I would be beat up like my mother. I viewed my life through the eyes of my paranoid-schizophrenic mother. Through meditation, I found that my father never intended to hurt me; the problem was between the two of them. In my illusion of needing to survive, I had reacted to the fear of being physically hurt.

Drugging me disempowered me and gradually increased my insanity; I had to give up all drugs to stay alive. I found that Bipolar Disorder is a way to run away from reality, much like an alcoholic drinks to run from reality. Taking the Valium the psychiatrist gave me also became a way not to face life or my anxiety. Replacing my unhealthy reactions with sane ones allowed my inherited mental illness from my mother to come to the surface, to be recognized for what it is, not facing life on life's terms.

My mind can release all the fears, resentments, anger, and shame of my past and be enhanced with the love inside that can now surface to replace my old dysfunctional life. Learning healthy behaviors to supplant my Bipolar Disorder activities was a major step. Now, I have the ability to live a healthy, empowered life free of what others think or say I should be, how I should act to make others' lives easier, or have a medical condition through a false premise of a medical protocol.

I could not be honest with myself while drinking alcohol and using prescriptions. I was irrational, immature, and living in fantasy. *Knowing* the truth did set me free. Today, I help clients find their answers in their subconscious with therapeutic regression therapy. Drugs prevent authenticity, I found; therefore, it is only a band-aid, as the real problem is still not addressed. However, when I became clear minded and rational, I could see myself acting out in extreme ways and could actually stop it.

Through my own self-searching, prayers and meditations, I applied methods to transform my fear-based history to a love-based life. I could move into the present. I needed behaviors that respond in love to my challenges or old past buttons. My clients and I found that the chemical imbalance returns to balance when a person has found their equilibrium. My Bipolar Disorder had been survival without any information of how to handle life or fear. It was a behavior and emotional problem, not a lack of Depakote.

My Bipolar Disorder was a childish, unconscious choice to live in fantasy. It became a choice to grow up. My withdrawals from Depakote took about four months of anguish. Edgar Cayce's readings said I could move beyond my condition. I could change my thinking and behavior to become loving, rational and logical. I could replace my old thinking and actions and not keep recreating the old patterns. Mind and mood altering drugs prevent being rational and clear minded. Discovering that they are only a band-aid was a new awareness. The real problem is still not addressed.

During my daily meditation, I heard the silent voice ask me, "Are you ready to move out of your Bipolar Disorder, like my mother could not come out of her prison of paranoid schizophrenia?" I thought a moment and said, "Yes." Prior to this, my psychiatrist had told me that alcoholism is not a choice, but mental illness is. I now understood, I had the opportunity to change my life if I choose.

With more than sixteen years of being off all prescription drugs and off alcohol for over thirty-two years, I have healed my life. It is blissful to have peace of mind and see the beauty around me. I do not have to relive the past ordeal anymore, but live in the present with authenticity and legitimacy. I have found

"Heaven on earth."

Learning to love myself and not look to others who cannot love themselves to save me made the difference. The love is inside. Other people, religions, or drugs called prescriptions cannot save me, because it is an inside job. Mental illness is an emotional problem. I do not need drugs to flee; instead, I found a spiritual/loving basis for my life to embrace, which created health. Currently, I gratefully enjoy each moment instead of replaying the past.

Now as an Internationally Board Certified Regressionist, I assist people to find the root cause of any illness, so they, too, can replace the negative energy with a loving resolution. Current medicine does not offer that option. My clients and I found that the substance imbalance returns to stability when a person has found their love within to balance their life.

Through my own self-searching, prayers and meditations, I have also used alternative methods to transform my fear-based history to a love-based life in reality. I found that when a person can release the root cause for their feeling, they do not need the symptoms of running away.

Now I have the ability to have a healthy, empowered life, free of what others think or say I should be, how I should act to make others' lives easier, or have a medical condition through a false premise of a medical protocol. Learning to love myself and not look to others who cannot love themselves to save me made the difference. Other people or prescriptions cannot save me because it is an inside job. The love is inside. Mental illness is an emotional problem, not a drugging problem. Replacing my dilemma with love from my heart works. I became healthy. My mindset moved into the "Now."

Drugging me disempowered me and gradually increased

my insanity; I had to give them up. My mind can release all the fears, resentments, anger and shame of my past and be enhanced with the love inside that can now surface. Turning to the present love that is within is the solution. That is the answer to move out of a fear-based life, which is labeled Bipolar Disorder. Then the chemical imbalance returns to balance.

Replacing my dilemma with self honesty from my heart works. Healing methods promoting rational thinking and behaviors, in addition to prayer and meditation, provided me with sane thoughts and the normal life I was pursuing. Bipolar Disorder is no longer a lifetime sentence.

Fortunately, my psychiatrist supported being off medications. However, medications affect each person differently; this might not be good for everyone.

Because of my decision of substituting a daily spiritual program replacing medication, it is now blissful to have peace of mind and see the beauty around me. This supports a healthy recovering body and experience. The person needs to stay vigilant in a new structure, balance and focus. Centeredness and groundedness in present thoughts, communication and current activities shows progress.

One piece of information that was so helpful I will share with you. The challenge of life as a human being is to *Be Present in the Now*. When you are in the moment, you will not think about a previous thought. If you stand outside of the moment, you judge the past and remember your old thoughts instead of being in the minute. Then you re-act to the old thought and you act as you did once before.

There is a way to reframe this. There are two words: Reactive and Creative that can rearrange your feelings. They both have the letter "C." Instead of continuing living as a re-enactment, realize there is no previous thought about it; you now create your future. Now, when you "C" things, notice they are the same word. Only the "C" has been moved! It is possible to see each moment clearly without a previous thought, and you can create who you are rather than who you once were. When you "C" things suitably, you become creative, rather than reactive.

Nothing is more natural than love. If you act lovingly, you will be acting naturally. In the right state of choosing to be in unity and wholeness in consciousness, in that holy moment you are in Divine Reality, or the Buddha mind. Maturity is a choice you must make every day, every minute. It must become the very purpose of your life.

You always have help from God. Listen to the silent voice within that gives guidance every moment, daily. The new directions will create Divine Reality. If you make the choice continually to listen from within, you have achieved the reason for your life.

Following my first news release that "Bipolar Was Not Forever," I replied to a woman in Pakistan who contacted me about her diagnosis of Bipolar Disorder. I want to include what I wrote her. She thanked me and heeded my information, recovering quickly in this case. When she realized it was a behavioral reaction, she promptly was able to address that. One morning, she even called me long distance to attend her wedding.

Dear Nancy,

You are going through a growing time, when the ego is telling you how bad it is. Why do you believe your head's messages from fear, when your heart is always full of God's love? God is spirit, not a person. Your choice is to focus on loving yourself and others or focusing on the past that has wounds, fears, pain and suffering. You can stay in the past trauma and drama or move your conscious focus onto the loving things and people you do have in your life with gratitude. This is what meditation helps you do, enlarge the love and peace in your life by raising your consciousness into higher, more positive vibrations of energy.

Life is a choice, which do you choose? Do you give up on yourself or to move into the reality of love? It is easier to stay in the pain because it is familiar. Yes, the Bach Flower essences would greatly help you. I use them with my clients. If you write out the negative messages most bothering you, I can send which essences will help move that energy. I can send you affirmations to support the essences. For starters, take Rescue Remedy. It will help to stabilize you for now. Put three drops on your tongue four times a day. And if you drink water, put three drops in your bottle of water and drink it throughout the day. Tell yourself each time you use the drops or drink the water, *I am at peace. All is well. I am loved and safe.*

You never go backwards in spiritual growth; you are at a new level of sorting out the disorder in your life. You have completed your past cycle and are starting a new one. It seems futile, but you have made growth to get to this point. Who will win your brain or your heart?

You are comparing yourself to others. They are just there to help you see your own reflection. Where do you need to change?

It sounds like you have to put together some activities and participate in them. That is how you develop healthy relationships. I can give you more help on this later. However, the more you love yourself, the more you can love others.

You are afraid right now of allowing your emotions out

from past trauma. Therefore, you are protecting yourself, you feel isolated, and your relationships are not working, as you do not have a relationship with yourself. Write out your feelings. When you drop those walls of protection, knowing God is in the "NOW" and there is no other time in reality, you are free of the past threats. When the love in your heart is free of the fear, it can fill your heart and body from head to toe.

Become aware that you are allowing others to take away your power, when you focus on them. To do this takes an inventory of all your fears, resentments, guilt, shame and anger. Then see your part of the dynamics. Where were you selfish, dishonest, fearful, self-seeking, and inconsiderate? Whom did you harm in all of this?

You are always the one who is harmed by selfish acts, dishonesty, fear, and self-seeking. You are being inconsiderate of yourself when you do not let your inner love take care of you and guide you in all parts of your life.

So give all these negative emotions to the universe. Burn your written list of them in a bowl, so they can leave to be healed. Replace the emotional space within, with love and grace, and you become a love-based person and not a fear-based person anymore. You substitute the positive for the negative. Then when new situations come up, you address it with the same understanding as they have come up to heal also. This is the process of healing.

Everyone goes through the same process. However, in each lifetime we get the lessons right for that time. Others may have already done this work in a past time or will still need to do this work. So focus on Nancy. Ask yourself, "What does Nancy want?" It is time to love the real Nancy inside.

The little girl inside needs to be parented with the love you never got growing up. She is still scared. When she gets scared, you act as if it is terrible. However, it is a sign to find the love inside and do nice things for you. Your little girl inside feels hopeless, this is being suicidal. Nevertheless, with the spark of love in your heart that is your divinity, you are never hopeless; just let it expand to fill you and others. I use a teddy bear to hug while I sleep, which for an old woman sounds funny. Nevertheless, whatever makes you feel loved, DO IT! You have to fix yourself; no one else can do this job. It is why you are on earth.

Devoting your life to love, which I call the spirit of love, is another definition for God. Find a definition that works for you. God has not created havoc; it was the Ego or separation from God or lack of love that created the problems. Returning to real love heals the problems; eventually you become one with God, and you are walking good, love, or God.

You send this love to others by your presence of love. I do offer to contribute to my relationship, but not because I feel guilty, have to, or for selfish reasons. As a good person it comes from my heart as an extension of the God inside going out to others. I am just the conduit.

God does not allow a useless disease like Bipolar to destroy you. You do that to yourself if your reject love. Anything not loving is of the ego. That part of you that stops the love in your life is by saying to yourself that you do not deserve it, are not good enough, and other untrue beliefs. Everything positive is of God.

You wrote a script for your life before you ever came to earth, with the lessons needed to heal your soul. That is why you are here. Now is the time to complete the healing. The ego stops you from seeing the light at the end of the tunnel, so you need faith. The script includes knowing you already have won. You already are healed; you already are perfect in the eyes of love. This is only a dream from which you will awaken.

Walk as if you only have good with you and do good for yourself and others. Forgive yourself and those in your life for needing this lesson. You are not a bad person and they are not bad people. They are acting out their parts for you to see where the healing is needed. You all agreed to act out these experiences for you to learn faith, trust, love, compassion, forgiveness and gratitude.

The big lesson is not to run away from love, but to embrace it. When you run away, you are in Bipolar. When you move towards being more loving to yourself and others, you are embracing love. It is about expanding energy; that is God. Eventually, all your love towards those people playing their parts in your life will merge into oneness. You have then come home to heaven on earth. You see the love in their hearts and realize their actions were to help you. They were just parts of your psyche needing to heal.

Blessings, Marilyn

Love Brings Sanity to Mental Illness

I have been declared sane after years of living in insanity. My mother was paranoid schizophrenic and my father was an alcoholic. There was no sanity in my growing up. I did not know I was not living in truth. The crisis, chaos and turmoil were normal to me. My mother's fear was passed on to me in the womb, I know today. Therefore, I arrived in this world already fearful from her experiences transferring to me. As a good child, I did what I was told and adopted behaviors for my reacting from fear for my survival.

My mother's mental frame of mind was my model of how to live my life. She had experienced sexual abuse and plenty of abandonment issues, including attending twenty-nine schools while growing up. Trying to function in her life, she stuffed her feelings, as she could be hurt again. She did not want to be vulnerable or maltreated again. She stayed within her heart with a big wall of protection, like the walls of a bank vault, and never emotionally ventured out to be real. She lived her life in this fantasy, thinking that if she did not address it, it would go away. Eventually, I learned that I was maladjusted to life. I was in full flight from reality and an outright mentally defective person, too. These unhealthy ways to live life resulted in a chemical imbalance in my body to sustain this life. My life was not in harmony.

Realistically, when you do not share the abuse, problems or harms with a counselor or appropriate person who understands this pain, it increases. It became a huge bubble of protection for safety, keeping out reality. I followed her silent way to handle my abuse. In addition, she taught me how to get what I thought

I needed, by being passively controlling in my life. On the surface, I looked good, while behind the scenes I took extreme measures to run from facing life, as she taught me. It took fifty years to realize I was a control freak, and I learned it from her.

My father's fears started at the age of five, when he was coming to America. He was under the threat of being killed leaving Russia. He drank to ignore his fears. As Mom got older, the doctors gave her medications. These stuffed her feelings, which prevented her from facing them and moving beyond the past. I was set up to be mentally ill, to drink, and to use prescriptions to run from reality.

Stopping my drinking and later stopping medications was a decision because the side effects were worse than the problems. I had to face the truth about myself. Fortunately, I found a psychiatrist who understood this condition. In explaining my mother to me, he told me that alcoholism is not a choice, but mental illness is. Today, I understand this.

There were steps to growing beyond my old learned reactions. My new way taught me to surrender to a higher power that could restore me to sanity. This allowed me to replace my fears with love as my new motivation in life. With my new spiritual life, my chemical balance returned.

Gradually, I had enough knowledge to stop my reactions and could come back in loving solutions when the old buttons were pushed after I was free of all toxic substances. Now, I substitute God's love for the medications. I can practice responding in my new loving and healthy ways. I can see what I am doing when I do not take any more medications. Challenges can continue for me to identify, however, I do not want to react, but I can handle these situations and move forward with healthier actions, today.

I was off Depakote for a while. When I returned home from a month's vacation with relatives in another state, I noticed a class on the East Coast I wanted to attend. I was exhausted from the long drive home from Colorado and really needed to stay home. However, my childhood did not allow me to rest from chores or sickness. I had to keep running. I had to do the next task, sick or tired, or else.

When I called in to reserve my place in the class, I realized something was wrong; I could not do that while medicated. The price for attending got higher and higher. Suddenly, I realized that the cost was climbing beyond $5,000 and this was going to be too expensive.

In meditation, I was told to call them back and cancel my class reservation. My head cleared when I made the call. I had not kept running, even when exhausted. The relief of coming into sanity was obvious to me. The moment I did this, my brain and reality was restored, immediately. Today, I can evaluate the situations that appear less often and act with appropriate responses for the situation.

Later, I had an episode where my paranoia schizophrenia surfaced to leave, emotionally. My anger came out like Mount Vesuvius. This is a good sign that the past energy is leaving. I allowed the anger to go, so I would be free to live in the present or be current in my life. The prescriptions had stopped my fearful feelings from flowing out or leaving, to be replaced for loving feelings. The medications had stopped my emotional growth, as I felt the little girl inside releasing the anger.

I have a healthy life today, in reality because I have not had a drink in thirty-two years, and I have not taken a prescription for sixteen years. I moved out of my bubble of fantasy. With many inventories to remove my past harms and future worries, my mind is focused on the "Now." That is reality. I no longer live my life based on my past or my mother's past. I have moved into the love of the moment and enjoy life as it comes.

My adventure has brought me many insights into life, our consciousness, and how to restore sanity. Dr. Scott Peck, the author of the book *People of the Lie*, says that the levels of mental illness are the levels of dishonesty with oneself. I vowed to be as honest as I could be, as I did not want to be like my mother.

I found that a higher power of love with forgiveness can replace the past abuse, difficulties and events. If I choose to change my mind and live in the presence of love, I find that *Love Never Fails*. I discovered that love is a choice and heals. I found my psychiatrist was right; mental illness is a choice. The choice is to live in reality and grow up or continue the past boogie men taking up space in my brain. It takes courage to face the darkness and turn on the light/love within my heart. This became my new basis for life.

Currently, I discovered the secret that was the underlying source of the mental illness in the family. My mother could not tell anyone that she had been molested. In those days, that was not talked about. That emotional experience was locked up inside her until she died. I carried that emotionally without even knowing about it until recently. I relived her life in that way. It took years later, sharing stories with the family, to reveal that she was the one, when the account was earlier told without any names.

I looked to her for help when I was molested. Her response to a five-year-old was, "Don't feel that way" as she walked off and left me standing alone. At that point I stopped feelings in my life. It took years of recovery and counseling to understand I had stuffed my feelings about everything from that point and was not living in reality while I had acted out the rest of my life, which continued the family secret.

With my continuing to release more negative emotions from sexual abuse for sanity, it was time to be ready to feel those. This break into reality was monumental. Nowadays I have a new honest basis for my life. We are only as sick as our secrets. Knowing the truth and expressing the anguish will set you free from the ego's protection of deceit.

John Forbes Nash, Jr., who won the Nobel Laureate in Economics, was depicted in the movie, *A Beautiful Mind*. In the end of the show, he is no longer plagued by his mental illness. His comment was, "I quit listening to the voices in my head." I also fired the voices and now listen to loving messages for others and myself. I have moved out my brain and into my heart. It is glorious to be free from the ego's messages that kept me in mental illness. Growing up is not for sissies.

A Simple Way to Raise Your Consciousness

Several years ago, a friend had a program at her home where we tasted water from different colored carafes. Each pitcher had a distinct flavor depending on the color of the glass container. The water in the blue pitcher tasted unlike the water in the clear, yellow, red, or green jugs. This led me to realize that I could change the consciousness of water.

Then several years later, I saw a movie called, *What the Bleep Do We Know?* It combined documentary-style interviews, computer-animated graphics and a narrative that offered a spiritual connection between quantum physics and consciousness. The plot follows the story of a photographer as she encounters emotional and existential obstacles in her life and begins to consider the idea that individual and group consciousness can influence the material world. Her experience illustrates the movie's thesis about quantum physics and consciousness.

This avant-garde movie included a segment about Dr. Masaru Emoto. It led me to a new consciousness about our planet's most precious resource. His photographs of water crystals impressed me. His work is revolutionary in researching water, which he documented in his books with photos of crystals.

This Japanese doctor of alternative medicine first featured his pictures in self-published books, selling over 400,000 copies internationally. *Messages from Water* and his second book, *The Hidden Messages in Water,* have images of water surrounded in positive words and environment and water enclosed in negative expressions and settings.

The pictures are self-explanatory, showing the resultant

stunning water crystal exposed to a wholesome television show, a Mozart symphony, or words as simple as *thank you* and *angel*. The consequential effects of water exposed to heavy metal music, microwave ovens, and cell phones were repulsive. Even words as "you make me sick" and the word *Satan* were more than hideous and revolting.

The human body and the earth are composed of mostly water. This presents a profound and quantum leap to how I have come to view life and my health. With this new understanding, it can influence the pollution of the earth. In addition, this is life changing to my body's health.

The body contains as much as 75 percent water, depending on your age and other factors. He believed that our thoughts, attitudes and emotions affect the environment. His research has implications that created an impact on personal health. Now, I can change the consciousness of the water within myself to a healthy level.

The Russian biophysicist and molecular biologist Pjotr Garjajev and his colleagues also explored the vibrational behavior of DNA. He found that language could influence your DNA. He experimentally proved that you could simply use words and sentences of the human language to produce a change. However, stress, worry or a hyperactive intellect prevent successful hyper-communication or the information will be totally distorted and useless. Therefore, reducing or elimination of all fears producing negative thoughts, actions or words is necessary for full trans-formation into positive energy.

This finally and scientifically explains why affirmations, hypnosis and meditation involving higher consciousness can have such strong effects on humans and their bodies. It is entirely normal and natural for our DNA to react to language.

Therefore, I set out to apply these ideas to my life. I was in counseling for many years, trying to achieve a healthier lifestyle. I had achieved some success improving my life from trauma, drama and addictions. I had the idea to place on my drinking water the words that could help transform my life. "Love and Gratitude" became the first words I faced inward on my bottle of water.

I learned that certain colors for my bottle had meanings. I wanted a clear blue or green bottle. Since green energy and that color are used in Pranic healing, I chose a green bottle for its curative and heath giving properties. I printed out the words "Love and Gratitude" from the computer. I placed the paper facing the water inward on the outside of the bottle with a rubber band to keep it in place. Using this as my drinking water, which came from the wells in Edgewood, Wash., was fortunate. My water district had won the national contest for the best water in the United States.

For several years, I found myself gradually growing into a more loving and grateful state of mind. I enjoyed feeling better, and my life and health were improving in many ways. I was changing my life. Using meditation, flower essences, and hypnosis to support this change, I could tell the difference in myself. My health was improving. In addition, my traumatic past was less of an issue in my daily living.

Then, through a fluke, I felt it was time to raise the consciousness of the words on my bottle. I knew the word "God" had the highest vibrations in our language through a spiritual class I attended. The book study using *Life and Teaching of the Masters of the Far East* by Baird T. Spalding said this word is the peak energy. Why not place the word *God* on my bottle? For the last several years, I saw more growth in myself as I was becoming more mature and adult like in my thinking and manner.

It is important to understand that energy shifts when new positive energy comes into your consciousness. Ultimately, I became very ill. I had pneumonia for several months. Since the negative energy is no longer sustainable, it has to leave. I lay in bed, sleeping around the clock while my body detoxed. There was no reason to see a doctor; I knew the old toxic past was leaving and the darkness inside had to go. In my imagination, I placed a light bulb inside each of my lungs, to bring light inside my body. It was time to change from the darkness of depression, a lifelong struggle. My inner light was emerging.

The next winter I had another experience of detoxing as this new energy was emerging in me. Being down another winter with pneumonia was not fun, but again, it was necessary to replace the old dark and negative energies with the incoming, loving vibrations. It has been a gradual shift in consciousness. With other work to support this rise in my awareness and understanding, my life has moved into the higher consciousness where I am not fearful, anymore.

The new energy from my God water comes into my consciousness to replace the earlier trauma and karma of the past. After years of counseling, 12-step groups, and Search for God study groups, all my work was

GOD

LOVE & GRATITUDE

actually bearing fruit. I moved out of the past into being present in the "Now." I have ascended out of the world of the third dimension and into the fifth dimension of unconditional love and grace. I am moving into the grace of God and coming into the presence of eternal love.

My Affirmations

I trust me.

I approve of me.

I let in affection.

I forgive myself.

I make the rules for me.

I enjoy life and have fun.

I take credit for what I do.

I see my reflection in others.

I am a member of the universe.

I create and develop my talents.

I talk to me, gently and lovingly.

I create an abundance of friends.

I love myself and the good in me.

I reward myself instead of punish.

I give myself what I want and

I nurture me with good food and good ideas.

PART FOUR
FINDING TRUTH

Letting Go of Fear is Faith

My fears kept me from having feelings. If I felt feelings, they would hurt and be painful. Therefore, I became an iceberg. I looked good on the surface, but underneath the fear ran my life. I was a schoolteacher with great evaluations; I won the auditions to solo with the Bellingham Symphony, and I was Valedictorian when I graduated from high school. No one knew about the pain and loneliness that I endured. I looked good while I was dying on the inside.

Most people have fear in their lives that stops them from having the life for which they have dreamed. It ran all parts of my life. I did not participate in life like others because of feelings of rejection, abandonment and apprehension. I played it safe so I would not get hurt emotionally, or physically. I became a good doormat and martyr. I felt like the sacrificial lamb for the family. In fact, I won an international writing contest with my piece, "All Time Victim."

I was walking fear from my childhood and marriage of domestic violence and abuse. This left me feeling like a victim. I did not feel I had any power in my life; I felt powerless.

Life got so dire in my marriage, I was trying suicide and my husband was trying to kill me. One night when I knew I would not get home alive in a manic car ride from a Canadian vacation, I prayed, "God, please help me, I really do not want to die." This spontaneous prayer was not from the hymnal as I was taught. It just happened on the spot.

It changed my life from fear to faith. He pulled off the highway and passed out over the wheel. The shoulder of the road was a safer place instead of our insane drive on the road home. Ultimately, I found myself in treatment for addiction. Realizing that I was addicted to the prescriptions from the doctors was a shock. I was told in treatment that I was a sick person needing to get well. What did that mean?

At the treatment center, I learned about needing a conscious connection with God, that I was sick and spiritually bankrupt. I had built emotional barriers to protect me in survival from my childhood abuse and was not consciously connected for God's love to nurture me.

I recognized that even though I had gone to church for fifty years, I was not living in faith. I even had a ten-year pin from Sunday School for my years of perfect attendance. As an adult, I had my children confirmed in our Lutheran Church. We looked good.

I found out I had been living in fear without any faith. I do not remember ever having a class at church or a sermon on "What is faith?" I was doing it my way, trying to survive, and it was not working. I was setting up my life to be safe, like ducks in the carnival shooting gallery. My plans usually did not come off the way I wanted. They fell apart and came back to bite me.

I learned that faith meant my work was to do what was needed and allow God to bring the results. What a shock to allow God to bring the results. That doomed my playing God in my life or with my family. Now I had a new employer, God. My life changed to "Thy Will Be Done." I had to allow my family to have their own concept of God and follow their own inner guidance.

This took faith; I had none.

My first attempt to try to walk in faith was while helping someone through a difficult time. I arranged for her medical help. I was hoping she would be able to follow through with her treatment and rehabilitation. I prayed, "God, I need faith for this one, Thy Will Be Done." The result was she did not have the courage to go for treatment. I had the pieces put together for her to walk through the door of the hospital. I was devastated that she could not proceed as I had arranged. However, I had to accept the outcome.

Again, I set up the planning for her treatment. I prayed, "God, I need more faith for this one. Here we go again." As more tests came up, I prayed for my faith to increase for the next bigger challenge. Later I realized that these were trials for me to begin applying more faith in my life.

I found partial faith does not work. I tested the waters. I prayed for a 10 percent faith to work. Next time, I prayed for 50 percent faith to manifest. I was still not completely buying this faith business. In each case, I could tell the 10 percent or 50 percent faith results were good and the rest fell apart. This was growing my faith. However, to get the best results, I had to make a decision for absolute faith.

Since then, it has been easier to surrender, totally, to God's way of arranging the results. I have to accept the outcome as His will. Surprise! The consequences will be better or just right. Recently, I hoped to visit my great grandson in Idaho. I thought that it was not going to come together. My schedule was too busy to make it possible. I gave up that I could make it happen.

With one unexpected phone call, the trip came together and I will not have to drive as far to see him. He will be visiting relatives in a closer town. Another good part was that my daughter would be there, so I will see her, too. The icing on the cake is that I just completed a portrait of him and I will be able to personally take him the painting and not have to mail it.

Wisdom came when I realized that I could not have fear and faith at the same time. Nowadays, I choose to do the footwork and have *Thy Will Be Done.* Learning God works in wonderful ways, I "Let go and Let God." It works out better than I can plan or put together.

Changing My Life into Gold

The Hermetic Philosophy

I attract all those seeking God and the truth;
those alone will find the art.
I am the Magnet-Stone of divine love;
attracting the Iron-hard men on the road to the truth.

I thought my life was in concrete and I did not know how to change it into something better. Isn't there a way for joy and happiness to fill my life? Since childhood, my life had been difficult. Going to college was a better time. However, when I married, gradually it was worse than my growing up. How do you get out of this dilemma? Am I doomed to live a life of being a victim and abused with no life of my own?

At one point, I heard about alchemy. It was concerned particularly with attempts to convert base metals into gold or to find a universal elixir. However, I did not understand the significance of turning metal into gold, except that I could be richer. What if I could turn my life into being worthwhile? I could transform myself into having value. What a dream!

Alchemy texts are secretive and written in a metaphorical code, filled with extravagant imagery. It is an ancient practice shrouded in mystery and secrecy. Its practitioner's purpose was to turn lead into gold, a quest that has captured the imaginations of people for thousands of years.

Alchemy was practiced in Mesopotamia, Ancient Egypt,

Persia, India, Japan, Korea and China. The start of Western alchemy generally is traced to ancient and Hellenistic Egypt, continuing through Greek and Roman times. It was the Medieval forerunner of chemistry, based on the supposed transformation of matter.

A spiritual way of life emerged through my decision to find a healthier lifestyle from my illnesses, addictions and trauma. In this search for finding the real me, I learned that many spiritual practices were not allowed in past times as the church found them to be blasphemy. These spiritual lessons and teachings became hidden in forms to disguise their real meaning. One example is the song for Christmas called "The Twelve Days of Christmas." It was written in England with hidden spiritual meanings as a catechism song, to help young Catholics learn the tenets of their faith. This memory aid was needed as being caught with anything in writing indicating adherence to the Catholic faith could not only get you imprisoned but killed.

Another instance of hiding secret knowledge has been in the Tarot cards. The tarot is a symbolic oracle that provides messages from our higher selves and the universe. This information comes to the inner person instead of through an organization or church. Therefore, the institution or tradition would not be necessary. This was threatening to authority if a person can acquire personal information, bypassing the religious leaders. For this reason, the cards have been rejected and demonized.

When I awaken to the secret code within Alchemy, I can transmute myself into a better person. I made the decision to restore my life into the love for which I longed. This would transmute my denseness into the bullion that shines like gold.

My life started with fear in the womb. My mother's fear from her lifetime of abuse transferred to me before I was born.

Socrates said, "The unexamined life is not worth living." Unraveling the elements that accompanied me throughout my journey has been revealing.

I always felt like an orphan from the time of my birth. Abuse began for me as an infant in a house of domestic violence. My father was an alcoholic and my mother was mentally ill. Later, she married a man more dysfunctional than my father and my life became more abusive, violent and insecure. Living in an impaired family did not allow me to feel loved or safe. Feeling alone and lonely, I never believed that I fit in anywhere.

My mother, being powerless and a victim, modeled what she knew. Because I did not want to be hurt, I tried to survive without being harmed. In my child's mind, *if my mother is hurt and I am no better than my mother is, then I deserved to be harmed too.* My inner, negative messages convinced me I would never be "good enough," be able to develop confidence, or find happiness.

Change only came after a lifetime of mental, spiritual and physical illness and emotional devastation. My bottom brought me to many death experiences. I knew I was dying, from a thirty-year marriage of domestic violence and rape, prescription drugs and alcohol. Since I have been close to death twelve times, it was time to find answers.

My husband and I stopped drinking for thirty days. Our trip to Harrison Hot Springs in Canada was our reward. He decided to have an evening cocktail to celebrate our pleasant trip. He became angry when I fixed my dress. Within minutes after his first drink, he raged about my actions. His sex addiction took over and the rest of the evening became a nightmare.

We ended up leaving the hotel at two o'clock instead of in the morning. He made me promise I would not get out before we got home. Because I was emotionally immature at that time, I agreed, as I did not want to be in a foreign country on my own. My wrathful husband drove like a maniac on both sides of the road and then stopped and parked in the middle. We almost had two head-on collisions. This time I knew I would not get home alive. Without thinking, I found myself saying, *God please help me, I really do not want to die.*

My husband pulled off the highway and passed out over the wheel. In the morning, he locked me in the car at the border station into the States. A short time later, he wanted a cup of coffee, so we stopped at a restaurant. In the restroom, my scared inner child wrote a note for the police to get me out of the car.

After leaving the restaurant, the sirens stopped us. Five police cars came to my rescue. Ultimately, I called my son to drive to Sumas, Washington, and pick me up.

Again, I found myself at my minister's house for safety while serving restraining orders. My husband ended up in Alcoholics Anonymous, and I ended up there too, after treatment. While I was at Puget Sound Hospital, I made the commitment to turn my life over to the care of God. I had already been in hell. This was a better option and my way out of suffering.

You must think you are not a good person, if you have to try so hard to be good, I heard from inside one Saturday morning. Miraculously, I heard the message in a new and different way. My illusion of looking good to others began to crumble at that moment. I saw a glimmer of my own internal goodness and looked forward to the future for the first time.

This kind of unmanageable life is the direct result of fear, without the ability to overcome it. I was running amuck from my fears and needed to change. Gradually, I came to realize that I was creating my own drama. I became willing to leave behind the tragedies. Finally, I understood I was my own worst enemy.

When I changed my attitude from one of fear and panic to loving others and myself, I created a life filled with caring people and positive experiences. This was the first day of a new life that I claim and enjoy today. This spiritual shift, from fear to love, drove me to find the truth about myself.

Major Issues I had to address and heal:

1. Abandonment from parents
2. Lack of nurturing to mature
3. Resentments
4. Fear
5. Guilt
6. Shame
7. Jealousy and envy
8. Behaviors
9. Relationships including Past Lives
10. Karma
11. Addictions including alcohol, prescriptions, co-dependency, sugar, smoking, etc.
12. Compulsive Behaviors and Obsessive Behaviors including workaholism, overachieving.
13. Mental Illness
14. Domestic Violence
15. Medical conditions (symptoms of separation from God)

Waking Up

Currently there are many spiritual teachings available that refer to a shift from the third dimension of duality to the fourth of God-Consciousness, and then into the fifth dimensions of living in a loving environment of peace and grace often called

Christ Consciousness. This shift is all about raising your energy, vibrations, and awareness. Moving into faith, new perceptions, and a higher consciousness is happening right now. I began to see that I was my own alchemist. The change happens within me.

I first heard the principle, "Everything is vibratory" when studying Edgar Cayce. It made sense to me in understanding God as spirit. It is all about vibrations. Everything is a vibrating energy in different planes, including your thinking about illness, scarcity, and even relationships. Higher vibrating energy is in good health, abundance, and loving relationships.

Dr. Max Planck supports that all physical matter is composed of vibration. The difference between the manifestations of the physical, mental, emotional and spiritual has a result simply from different levels of vibrating frequencies or power. In addition, Einstein proved that we could break matter down into smaller components and that, when we do, we move beyond the material realm and into a realm in which everything is energy. This is the Law of Vibration, a law of nature that states that nothing rests; everything moves and everything vibrates.

The vibrations range from the very negative, fearful ways of thinking that would be called a dense metal, metaphorically into the highest and truest thinking characteristic that is labeled gold. When you journey through all levels, you reveal yourself and find God. *In the Bible, this is moving up the emotional steps of consciousness termed Jacob's Ladder. My chart* shows the numbers for the vibrations on the stairs as they ascend into a higher pulsation often referred to as Christ Consciousness, fearlessness, unconditional love, or fifth dimension.*

Cayce states, *the vibratory force is the active principle all radiates from.* (#195-54) Therefore, the truth is that the dark,

---

* See Appendix page 187

denser energy in your body needs to be brought into the lighter and higher vibrations. Darkness is separation from God and the amount of light within is your intimacy with God. The goal of life is enlightenment—becoming the light of God. Cayce also states, *Matter is the expression of spirit in motion.* (#262-78) This is the journey on earth and this is the path to return home. It is moving into more light of an elevated vibration of consciousness. This is the meaning of being the Prodigal Son returning to the oneness of spirit that is our home.

I can move into being at *cause* in higher energy or spirit. When you are willing to change your vibrations to a higher state, you are telling the universe that you are very ready; it is purposeful and intentional.

Now I keep in mind *why I am here* during this particular time on earth. Surprisingly, I remember that I agreed to participate in this astounding experience of raising my vibrations, which then raises the vibrations of the planet. I agreed to transform any darker and lower vibrating energies. This means I am cooperating with my soul as a team. No longer am I acting like a victim who is having a non-voluntary experience because I volunteered for this before I came to earth.

The point of attraction attracts like energy. The more fear one has of anything, the more a vibrational match there is. When I withdraw my attention from it, I no longer have vibrational access to it. The more I am in gratitude for the gifts received, and say, "Bring on more," more will come.

I had to change my focus one evening from anguish. I went to the war movie, *Behind Enemy Lines*. I agreed to see the show to impress a boyfriend who wanted to see it. This was a time when I was becoming more sensitive and could not take the shooting and fearful suspense. I found myself leaving the theater, telling my friend that I would pick him up when the film was over. Changing my focus stopped the anxiety and uncomfortable feelings.

My guidance system comes from my emotions. Moreover, since everything is vibration, my guidance system is the method for understanding what I am creating in this moment. Emotional frequencies are just vibrations. In essence, what I am learning to do is to manage my energy vibration by managing my feelings. If you feel good, you are doing God's will. This is changing the density of the metal into gold, emotionally.

As my vibrations rise, my perceptions change. In addition, people and interests in my life change. I then begin to attract new friends who are more in harmony with my new perceptions. I have experienced this several times over the years.

I had had a high school friend for forty-five years. We had been best friends and kept up our companionship through marriages, divorces and life activities. I relied on my friend for support through my difficulties in life, thinking of her as the sister I never had. She relied on me, too.

I began my spiritual journey after leaving a treatment center for addiction to prescription drugs. Shortly after treatment, I was on my own because I had a divorce. Holidays were not easy times without a family. She always included me for holiday dinners and to join her family for a day at her beach home.

We remained friends, but gradually things changed. Her new husband was not accepting of me. Gradually, he became very angry and did not like me. I was changing into loving ways and new values. At one point he became so hostile to me, I was not eager to continue visiting. When I declined to endorse some legal papers, he told me that he never wanted to see me again. It was a test for me to follow my new principles for my current values. I could not sign for something that I saw as a potential danger for two innocent children. I did not feel right about the circumstances that the papers would incur.

My grief and loss were heavy. However, I needed to remove myself from toxic situations and not support a situation that was against my higher principles. I realized that the universe took me out of a relationship that no longer matched my present principles.

Everything is vibrational. Therefore, although it may not appear to be so, I was the one pulling the plug on my relationship, even when it appears to be my friend's husband when he said we never want to see you again. *For without passing through each and every stage of development, there is not the correct vibration to become one with the Creator,* said Edgar Cayce. (#900-16)

In addition, Cayce says, *"All strength, all healing of every nature is the changing of the vibrations from within, the attuning of the divine within the living tissue a body to Creative energies. This alone is healing ... it is the attuning of the atomic structure of the living force to its spiritual heritage."* #1967-1

If you have an uncomfortable situation, I found a helpful hint. Forgiveness is another way to raise my energy and spirit into more brightness. Forgiving everyone from the past, present, and even those who come into my future has brought a higher consciousness.

A conviction to live and triumph over unhealthy emotions allows me to discover hope and faith. Now, with courage, I can proceed so my spirit can rise above the negative energy called ego, the devil, or Satan. You, too, can rise above the lower denser vibrations of energy of your character flaws, to live forever in higher emotions of joy that the resurrection of Easter represents.

If something you want is not coming to you, it always

means the same thing; you are not an energy match to your own desires. This means the Universal Laws are operating in your life. These invisible laws of the universe are the basis for our growing into the higher consciousness. I find that the universal laws work, whether I say the right words or believe the right ideas or not. Speeding down a road near my home years ago, I saw the speed limit sign. It dawned on me that there are other laws in the planet that operate, whether I know about them or not. When I ignore the laws beyond the worldly, material plane, I receive those consequences too, even if I am not aware of them.

I came across a cartoon with the Ziggy character. The drawing showed Ziggy in a puzzled state, looking up at the ceiling saying, "No one taught me the rules for living." I identified with the absence of this important information.

Universal Laws are those laws for living. Some of them are Law of Cause and Effect, Law of Abundance, Law of Love, Like Attracts Like, and Law of Attraction. When you become familiar with the laws, your life becomes content and revolutionizes. You now are cooperating with the universe. Changing your behavior and thinking results in different outcomes as you combine forces with the laws of nature. They are laws of love. When I align with the love in the universe, I move into a higher consciousness of the loving universe that supports me in all things. I become the gold at the end of the rainbow.

Compulsive behaviors such as overachieving, workaholism and perfectionism can repress my emotional growth and stop the energy from moving. Recently, a famous television star announced that she ate 35 pounds of macaroni and cheese to cover her depression when a passionate project bombed. Is that a major cause of people being overweight, their unexpressed emotional pain? Food can easily hold back feelings in the same way as alcohol, prescriptions and other toxic substances.

When I feel better emotionally, the more I allow my alignment with Source energy. This alignment includes the cells in my body. Therefore, this affects my health as well. During days and weeks of daily participation in meditations, my clarity and better health did happen. Listening, relaxing and breathing in a higher consciousness of love makes a difference.

Eventually, with daily focus upon breathing and releasing resistance, the Law of Attraction synchronizes me into better-and-better-feeling thoughts. The more good-feeling thoughts in my focus, the more the cells of my body can animate. I am an energy being affected by energy/God. This is why energy healing, vibrational medicine, and hands on healing are so effective.

I noticed a marked improvement in clarity, stamina and vigor as I literally breathe into wellbeing with feelings of appreciation, eagerness and joy, confirming that I have released resistance and are now allowing health.

Dr. Gerber in his book, *Vibrational Medicine,* asserts that, "interestingly, many of the healing modalities discussed in this book [his book] are often less expensive and considerably less toxic or risky than conventional medical and surgical methods." He continues, "In the future, homeopathic remedies and flower essences may be recognized as useful for treating various chronic ailments."

This is the world of duality with a density of darkness from the ego's fear. We have free will in making a choice between the ego, which is represented by the dense metal and God/love that is symbolized by gold. As I choose love to heal, I come out of that paradigm of the lower third dimension density of duality and rise into higher vibrations of energy that are lightness, transparent, and brightness in oneness. This is the right use of free will.

In accessing the vibration that matches the Source, I return into the oneness with the totality of spirit, what we call the Holy Spirit of God. I am a whole spirit with universal love gluing back the wounded parts of my soul. The Universal Law of Attraction—Like Attracts Like—works in many ways of our lives; this is its most profound facet. Altering and transforming my vibrations back to those of the Creator's love. I then return home. This is the great inner urging of our soul. This is the ultimate alchemy.

"We are an energy field. It is possible to move your energy from lower energy into higher vibrations of loving feelings."   ~Marilyn L. Redmond

"LOVE, which is the same energy as light and the essence of all souls, is the most powerful force in the cosmos. LOVE-LIGHT is the key to resolving all conflicts and feeling peace within!"
                    ~ Matthew channeled by Suzanne Ward

"In the presence of the dominion that God gave us, there are no problems, nothing of sin, lack, or disease to be over-come." He also says that "...if we can discover within ourselves the nature of spiritual power, we have found the great secret of life."   ~Joel S. Goldsmith

"Electricity or vibration is that same energy, same power, ye call God. Not that God is an electric light or an electric machine, but vibration that is creative is the same energy as life itself."   ~Edgar Cayce

Physics and Spirituality Merge

My life is like an iceberg, where the larger part is not perceptible below the surface. With my new understanding and awareness, I came to understand that what I do not see is running my existence. It became time to move beyond the observable focus on form into the formless of the unseen called spirit, love, or innate consciousness which vibrates at different rates.

Historically, in the writings of Aristotle and other scholars, matter was defined as being in itself formless, but it could receive form and substance. Today, matter is defined scientifically as waves of energy that are visible to the human eye and what makes vision possible.

However, with current discoveries, the evidence that there is energy vibrating beyond the range of the human eye also exists as we learn about ultraviolet rays. This light is invisible because it is not perceivable by our normal senses. Light not perceivable is called *ultraviolet* light. It is electromagnetic radiation with a wavelength shorter than that of visible light, but it is longer than soft X-rays. The name means "beyond violet" — *ultra* is the Latin word for "beyond," and violet is the color of the shortest wavelength of visible light.

Cayce links the pulsating energy seen as light in tangible third dimension as the basis for all life. He states that it is also the unseen energy that is found in the environment and is the same as the energy of light we label God, the unseen. *"And as the electrical vibrations are given, know that Life itself — to be sure — is the Creative Force or God, yet its manifestations in man are electrical — or vibratory. Know then that the force in nature that is called electrical or electricity is the same energy ye worship as Creative or God in action."* #1299-1

This understanding brings us to realize that there is light or energy in everything in the world. Most people know Genesis 1:3 that says, "And God said, Let there be light: and there was light."

Cayce said, "God moved and said, 'Let there be light' and there was light; not the light of the sun, but rather that of which, through which and in which, every soul had, has and ever has its being. For in truth ye live and move and have thy being in Him." (#5256-1)

I realized that light and love is labeled God, Creator, spirit, or a term that fits your understanding of a higher power. Other terms are Creative Intelligence, Creative Forces, Spirit of the Universe, and Source. "God is—God is light—God is love." This state of consciousness is unconditional love, also called the Christ-Consciousness, where there is no fear, and wellbeing and good health abound. "The Christ Consciousness ... is the only source of healing for a physical or mental body" brought this together for me by Cayce. The Bible says, "If any man be in Christ, he is a new creature." (II Corinthians 5:17). Therefore, our energy can move into a higher range, which is the metaphysical gold of the alchemist.

This universal intelligence exists by whatever term you choose to use. Therefore, this light/energy vibrates in alignment with the beneficence of the universe brings light to the darkness and offers life and harmony. The light in the highest vibrations beyond our physical vision becomes the substance once sought after by those who believed in a way to prolong life indefinitely and transform base metals into gold. This fits the definition by alchemists—a life-prolonging elixir, a universal cure for disease, and a universal solvent alkahest.

As this light moves down through the dimensions, vibrations of color changes and the distance between the particles becomes more compact. Therefore, the compressed particles cannot move as it did in its original source of a higher dimension. This feels like separation from the power of light and brings darkness or the absence of light ultimately, if not remedied. Emotionally, this becomes selfishness, fear and resentments; this medically is called poor health, dis-ease, or death. This state of vibration often is labeled the devil or Satan by religious organizations. Rather than a foe, darkness is the lack of light at varying low degrees of energy within us.

In lower dimensions, it is unavailable to produce health. The motivation behind this lower energy actually comes from our negative and harmful thoughts, words, actions, and toxic environment. This negativity found in lower vibrations creates egotistical, unharmonious, and blocked body energy. When people act from this consciousness, they project it to others while draining themselves of needed energy for their own wholeness.

Blaming a devil or Satan for misery or poor health is pointless because I brought it on myself through neediness and fear. Fear creates a dark blanket, usually called the veil, that prevents the raising of energy. By moving beyond fear, I found the light. With this understanding, I assumed responsibility for my life and health. This is based on the universal law that "Like attracts like."

The spirit of God is forty octaves above my perception. When my inner energy is not in alignment and harmony with the supremacy of illumination, illness is the result. When my actions and communications emerge from kindness and patience, a higher frequency with light and love, joyful rewards appear. Mystics call this high inner power the God within.

Most people have heard of the Golden Rule. In the New Testament it states, *You shall love your neighbor as yourself*, in Matthew 17:17. When I apply these principles to my life, I send my inner love to cooperate, merge and send out my inner love from my heart. I feel happiness, bliss and contentment in my good health and prosperity; I project it to others. This is peace on earth.

People were less sophisticated 2,000 years ago. Terms to understand the message used images, stories and metaphors called parables. When the Bible was first written, it referred to the *light of God* and *the Father and I are one*. This means the God/light within. However, at that time in history, they were not aware of the invisible energy creating them that is in all things. God became a physical being with a name because only the physical world was in their awareness.

In addition, the church at the time only allowed their dogma to be lawful. Therefore, if you interpreted the scriptures differently, it was against the church and often the law. This blasphemy quandary was similar to the times of the Inquisition later. Therefore, people were careful how to phrase their message. Using parables and stories masked the message behind the story, thus saving imprisonment or torture. This was referred to in *He that hath ears to hear, let him hear.* Matthew 11:15

Lastly, the common person did not read, and there were no Bibles until 1454. The Bible was read to the people in Latin. Mass was not spoken in English until the early 1960s. If the religious followers were allowed to think for themselves, there would be no need for priests and a church. If they realized that it was an inner source within and not an outward person that would save them, there would be no need for organized religion, dogma and its rituals. The idea of a savior was a church idea.

In our scientific and psychological world of today, it is time for a new perception that is more accurate to understanding the allegories and symbols. *A Course in Miracles* says that words are symbols of symbols. I first understood this thirty-one years ago, when reading the words of the Bible one morning before leaving for work; the words stood out from the page to show the spirit behind the words. The Bible did the best at that time to describe something not able to be seen—a beneficent, benevolent energy that sustains us all in life.

People gave words to this indescribable creative force. Seeing the physical world as a reflection of inner consciousness was not understood at that time in history. It is time to modify the perception of God because quantum physics/science has revealed more observant awareness about life.

Science has developed into a more sophisticated knowledge today. "I am the light of the world: he that followeth me shall not walk in darkness, but shall have the light of life." John 8:12 directly addresses moving from the denseness of a lack of light of God. God has many terms and synonyms. Life and God are interchangeable.

Religion, science and holistic health are talking about the same thing. By not separating church from science or health, truth-seekers can unite with the Law of Vibration. In Einstein's Theory of Relativity, energy is related to matter and the speed of Light. This is Einstein's famous $E = mc2$ equation.

Science has a newer understanding from quantum physics, which is bringing the link and relationship closer to identifying the unifying nature of light. The spirit within manifests as a human being. Bringing this invisible vibration to the visible will be shortly demonstrated in science. Physicists at Imperial College London claim to have cracked the problem using high-powered lasers and other equipment now available. "We have shown in principle how you can make matter from light," said Steven Rose at Imperial.

When two frequencies are brought together, the lower will always rise to meet the higher. A misaligned piano string is altered to be in tune by striking a tuning fork and the string matches that vibration for the correct timbre. The string then raises its resonance to the same rate at which the fork is vibrating. The sound wave created by the Ohm Tuning Fork works like kinetic energy to move disharmony and tension from the body while restoring a sense of wellbeing.

The light that is denser and tangible on planet earth is the same force that people refer to as God, Creator, or Higher Power. This new perception will acknowledge that the lower finite visual matter and extended higher vibrations into infinity are the same. This verifies the idea that we are one light or one in love. Thus, we can rise up in vibration into a higher consciousness of love.

The words to the song, "This little Light of mine, I am going to let it shine," refers to the inner light that is high energy, a higher power within. Daniel 5:14 said, "I have even heard of thee, that the spirit of the gods is in thee, and that light and understanding and excellent wisdom is found in thee." Cayce brings it together when he states, "The spirit of light, of hope of desire to know truth, must be greater than that man has called scientific proof, yet it is the science of light, of truth, of love of hope of desire, of God."

In her book, *Love Without End,* Glenda Green explains that your love brings forth your life. This can be further explained as love brings forth God or God brings forth love. There is always an ocean of an infinite supply of light; this light is power, energy, or the Creative Forces. This invisible life-giving force is omniscient, omnipresence, and omnipotent.

These attributes are always adapting and aligning with loving energy manifesting health and wellbeing. This is the river of life. This life force is energy that flows to all who are open to receiving. This connects the unseen of religion called God to the visible of science. All you have to be is the love that you are. Then everything will line up around you like a magnet.

If you want to find the secrets to the universe, think in terms of energy, frequency, and vibration. Tesla.

Universal Laws are My Tools for Alchemy

Finding the process to transform my life is the ultimate goal. I found that a spiritual life is exactly my answer. Transcending my old life into one that is based in truth and spirit will provide the ingredients for this change. Over time, I found these to be the Universal Laws.

A universal law is an unbreakable, unchangeable principle of life that operates inevitably. These operate in all phases of our life and existence, for all human beings and all things. They work regardless of your belief system, I found. Each culture has its own terms for spirit and divine love.

Edgar Cayce, the Father of Holistic Health, said, "...in compliance with laws all things become possible with one complying to such laws..." Universal Laws are the highest way to achieve this. When you draw on the laws in your daily life, the Creative Force universally called God works with you. Love is a choice.

In not just complying with a law, it is making you one with the purpose of the universe. This means transforming to selfless rather than selfish. This allows you to release your fears, doubts and resentments and you move beyond them into the complete love of the universe. Jesus told this message 2,000 years ago, and now there is an openness, understanding, and consciousness for transformation. My only way is up when I cooperate with the universal laws!

The Universal Laws are laws of truth and love. I had to move from my head into my heart. I had to plant the seeds of love and peace within to bring results into my life. My life has become calm, peaceful and caring instead of my old life. I move from lower consciousness of metal or childishness into a higher one of gold or maturity.

What are some of these laws? Like Begets Like, Laws of Increase, Laws of Attraction, The Power of Expectancy, and Laws of Cause and Effect are basic ones. When I change my principle from deceit to honesty, the universe immediately is on my side for the reason that I have chosen to work in accord with it. I am returning from the metal basis of my life into the gold or god/goddess that I am. I am returning home. This allows me to move back into my inheritance of being created in the image of God. I am a Christed being releasing my human characteristics.

Love heals all things. No matter what kind of condition, situation or relationship I am addressing, bringing love to it will change it, lift it, or transform it. Love is the presence of God; God is love. It will transform anywhere, anytime, any condition, and any situation to which you apply it. When you bring this power to yourself to recognize and love that source within you, you open the gates to share yourself, your talents, your life, and abundance with others.

The practical application of this is to understand that each difficulty shows me the past pattern that has created the current problem. I need to bring love to the situation, person or place. As I do, love will eliminate the pattern or change the situation. I become transformed. The undesirable condition will no longer have a reason to exist, so it will be resolved.

I found a simple way to change this around. First, find the message. Keep it neutral and do not judge the situation. It becomes a lesson like being in school. Second, I find the feeling. By going into a relaxed, meditative state, I release the tensions in my mind and body by breathing out. Noticing my feelings about the situation brings my answers. I experience these feelings. Thirdly, I bring love to it. By accepting these feelings, I am aware of how to bring love.

This worked for me several years ago. I needed to replace my skylight in my home. The roofing man, who came to do this, did not confer with me as to the style of the skylight to be replaced. He assumed I would take any model he put in. However, the one he installed had a heavy ugly bar across the center, which stopped the view. In addition, I felt like I was imprisoned when it was installed. I was informed that the company who manufactured the skylight could not get the material large enough for an eight-foot single sheet skylight. The roofer told me there was a law that prevented one that large without a bar from being installed because something might fall from the sky and the bar would break the fall. I was angry.

All I wanted was one like I had had for many years and enjoyed the view. The local building office informed me there was no such law as he laughed. I also found that materials are available for this large size without going to Europe. I had been lied to by both men. Fortunately, a contractor friend I knew took me to a factory in another town where I could get another skylight like the one I was replacing.

The message was that my little girl inside me was fuming that she was not getting her way. The feeling was of being victimized and bullied. In my meditative state, I realized I would have to bring an adult approach to the subject instead of playing the victimized little girl. I stayed to the facts that there was no such law. I arranged for the replacement to come from the other manufacturing company. I agreed to pay extra for the correct one to replace the one I did not want, that had been installed without my approval and confirmation.

The roofer was not happy to have the unwanted skylight on his hands, but I did get what I wanted. Now several years later, I am so happy that when I sit in my hot tub, I can see the sky, moon and clouds completely without the unattractive bar in the way of the view. This was a lesson of several for me, to not be bullied and to step up into a mature response. Through the process of the controversy and compromise, I grew in self-esteem and felt empowered. I grew from the metal into the gold.

Since the Universal Laws are the basis of the order of the universe, as I make them a part of my life I can come to perceive that order. Remember that all I see in the world is a reflection of me. When I allow the laws of love to govern my mind and apply them, the order appears with wonderful feelings and a sense of common sense, sanity and wisdom. I become rational and stable as an adult.

Tools for Aligning with the Universe

There is one more component to moving my energy higher into the gold desired by an alchemist. I found the golden bullion within through consciously and completely aligning with the universe. "The physical body is an expression of your energy. However, when you clear the energy, because you are energy first, the physical body will soon follow. If you change your energy or vibration, the physical body will manifest the change. If there is something that you desire and it is not coming to you, it always means the same thing. You are not a vibrational match to your own desire."

~Abraham-Hicks

Many tools are available to help align your energy into the higher vibrations. One way to achieve the higher consciousness that is most helpful is by our language. It is suggested to focus your thoughts on what you *want*, not on what you *don't* want. Words themselves have vibrations.

Loving words spoken sweetly are nurturing and assist them in achieving balance. In addition, I found selected spiritual reading and channeled material to lighten my heart and mind is helpful. Conversely, not only does yelling harsh words to anyone destroy their balance, but also for the balance of the ones who yell. The yelling becomes returning memories in low vibrations. Less intense words also have vibrations, so choose your words carefully to benefit those to whom you speak, write, and yourself.

Dr. Emoto, in his research with water crystals, found that destructive words including killing, racism, rapist, and other negativity words undergirded consciousness lowering vibrations. LOVE/LIGHT is the key to resolving all conflicts and to feeling peace within.

Reiki, tuning forks, Chinese herbs, and many other ways to raise your energy are supportive in aligning to a higher consciousness. Other ways to raise my consciousness is through the use of flower essences. They are pure energy that transforms my negative emotions into the higher range of light/love. In addition, other homeopathic remedies are more useful than toxic medications to keep my energy higher.

The priceless tool is meditation. Prayer with meditation is one way to move into an altered state of consciousness where this change can occur. Raising your focus into the higher consciousness of your heart and beyond the Ego is the meaning of prayer. This simple way is always available to set free the barriers that are blocking off the sunlight of the spirit from your life. It needs space to expand. Letting go of self-created barriers of survival creates space to fill you with expanding love. In a higher focus, I allow the grace of God to increase and grow. My divinity is in my heart.

When I move into a higher vibration, I am ready to receive spiritual gifts of guidance, directions and information. Meditation and/or hypnosis to heal the damage at a subconscious level brings a complete healing. To correct my actions, thoughts and motivations are the purpose of my life on earth.

In my new awareness and openness, new results flow to me and manifest from spirit. In this change of awareness, my life advances into golden results. This is the meaning of Matthew 6:33, "But seek ye first the kingdom of God, and his righteousness; and all these things shall be added unto you." This is the goal of the alchemist.

I Am the Gold

Levels of consciousness are forever rising. Some call this progression a hierarchy. Love is the highest power in creation; it is the universal elixir of the alchemist. It is the supreme law whereby you throw off the bonds of separateness and perceive the great spiritual unity in which we have our fundamental essence. Happiness is a function of releasing your wants and desires for 'Thy Will Be Done.' I am then accepting the love within and sharing it. I become a channel of love, the highest vibration. It moves me into the highest realization labeled unconditional love, Christ consciousness, or grace.

The Law of Love is the most important of all laws; it is the creative force of all life. The impressive power of Love in the Universe is the glue-like energy waves that hold us together and bring us into Oneness, where we feel our own divinity and our own empowerment. "Therefore, if any man be in Christ, he is a new creature: old things are passed away; behold, all things are become new." 2 Corinthians 5:17

    I am free—free from fear and the past. I am happy, joyous and in gratitude in the presence of love. It is in that sacred moment that the Ego defers to the Father, leaving only Him. In that moment, form becomes formlessness and God meets God. I Am that I Am. I am the pot of Gold at the end of the rainbow.

Archangel Michael,
drawn as he described it to me
after seeing him appear to me in Spain

What is Innocence?

There are many perceptions about innocence. It is often said we are born with a clean slate. This common view is people are born without tribulations. Conversely, many believe that people are born unworthy. The other side of the discussion is that a child is born unworthy, with past experiences called karma, or there is divine providence that we address in this life from past lives. These opposing opinions have been an accepted controversy for many therapists, philosophers and theologians. Which is the truth? This has been a debate for years.

I have, fortunately, had to grow up from the emotional age of three years as an adult with seven years of college. As a retired schoolteacher, teacher in colleges, and now internationally board certified for regression therapy, IBRT, I am working as an international spiritual counselor, speaker, columnist and author. Rather than knowledge, it is from "knowing the truth" does set you free. I am fearless today and free from the ego's ruining my life. It has taken thirty-two years of self searching, meditation and counseling to find the answers.

Understanding the dynamics of consciousness from personal experience is unique. This needs to be addressed. It is not only from this life that that you are evolving. All my writing, counseling and speaking is to enlighten people how to overcome their past conditioning in this life and from past lives, called karma. The behavior, thoughts and feelings of a young child and how they respond are being played out from not only their present but from prior lives.

There is a pattern of behaviors, positive and negative, being put into balance by the child, unconsciously. Science observes the measurable and visible aspects of life. Many scientists have varying answers for altruistic or selfish behavior of toddlers. This sets up people to think they are supposed to act a certain way when it is not normal for all. Using data to put them all into the same box is not realistic. This is how science sets up people to behave a certain way when it is not usual. Everyone is an individual with his or her own experiences. We are not rubber stamps of each other. Each child handles the activity differently for his own circumstances and history. They are individuals.

Science explains their data by putting children all into the same box. This is not realistic. A number of researchers argue that children are selfish until they are socialized; they acquire altruistic behaviors only as childhood progresses, and they are rewarded for following civilization's rules, or punished for breaking them. This is generalizing that all children act a certain way to life experiences. To base research experiments onto everyone is generalizing and not seeing each as individuals with their own personality and path for growth. If this were true, we would all have the same life to live.

Witnessing my own twin grandsons, while babysitting one day, became a special event. Robert was playing with plastic measuring spoons on the kitchen floor. His brother, Ryan, wanted to play with them, too. Robert nicely passed them to Ryan. He received the spoons calmly, played with them for a short time, and returned them as nicely as he received them. They were still not walking at the time, but crawled around the house into the kitchen, enjoying the kitchen utensils for play. Pattern of behaviors—positive and negative—come into balance by the child, unconsciously. It is a unique behavior to that child. How they react or respond is their own way to approach life from their instinct.

Science observes the measurable and visible aspects of life. It is not rational to put everyone in the same box of behaviors. Spirituality explains the unseen aspects of the consciousness or soul of the child. In this life there is a choice to have an opportunity again to bring your life into a balance of love, and merge into the eternal spirit of the universe.

These lessons continue throughout our lives. As we grow, the learning continues. Gradually, the old behaviors from fear or lack are changed into responding in love. As the child grows, if his/her awareness has not happened, then life becomes unmanageable or unbearable. It often takes a huge crisis to look at what is not working anymore. If we grow beyond our old patterns, we develop and mature. The right challenge is right in front of us. It can come from early in life or from a past life, finally ready to be addressed. Life is a progressive series of opportunities to change your past into a new understanding and in a loving resolution.

Each experience is the ability to transform your life into a better one, thereby eliminating the past influences. There is no right or wrong behavior. That is a judgment. There is a bigger story. I am fortunate to have had the ability to grow up from the emotional three-year-old into an adult with the right education to understand the dynamics involved. Understanding the energy of truth does set me free. I am fearless today and free from my ego.

I have almost died twelve times in this life, to be able to explain this evolution of spirit within. I have grown beyond my past. My life has transformed into living in what feels like heaven on earth.

Spirituality clarifies the unseen consciousness or soul of the child. It is the life force where again you have an opportunity to restore balance. This makes it possible to merge into the eternal spirit of the universe. It has an inner focus rather than the outer focus by science. Scientists seem to apply right and wrong ways to reacting in activities; that is judgment. There is no bad behavior. Every act is a path towards growth.

There are several keys to moving into the innocence of a child that society is attaining at this time in history. Life has complex layers of current living experiences, and those from past life experiences, which need to come into balance. "My little children, of whom I travail in birth again until Christ be formed in you." Galatians 4:19. This Bible verse explains it simply. We continue to return until we grow into our Christ Consciousness. Therefore, what the child is doing is part of a larger picture for their lessons and maturity. We are purifying our souls for innocence.

Most people know the Bible verse, "But when Jesus saw it, he was much displeased, and said unto them, Suffer the little children to come unto me, and forbid them not: for of such is the kingdom of God" Mark 10:14.

The Bible was written over 2,000 years ago, before people were sophisticated in science to understand vibrations, energy and Quantum Physics. An interpretation of this passage with new understanding could be helpful. We are His children seeking love, which is His kingdom.

Jesus is our example of unconditional love, where there is no judgment, prejudice or fear. He ascended into the spiritual kingdom after he was crucified from his personality of anger, guilt and shame. He cleansed his soul of all negative thoughts, words or actions while in the desert. He resisted temptation from the tempter, and remained loyal to the love of his heritage. That is another way to understand innocence, virtue and purity. He cleansed his soul. When we move into the kingdom of God, we are virtuous and without any negative energy in our consciousness. We return to our source of love.

Our lives are about moving higher into an energy that is above the trauma, drama and turmoil of a third dimensional life. Moving up in consciousness is called awareness or awakening. In the Bible, it is called Jacob's Ladder. I depicted the stairs in an art piece to a higher consciousness, called heaven in my book, *Paradigm Busters, Reveal the Real You.* *

The earthly material world distracts us from the spiritual inner world within us all. With an inner experience and perception, we become selfless without any selfish motivations or plans. When raising our vibrations from a lower one into a higher consciousness of love, we have grown beyond the earthly standards. "Little children, keep yourselves from idols. Amen." 1 John 5:21

Consciousness is the spirit within us all. When that is cleansed, we have moved into the kingdom of unconditional love. Our consciousness has moved up in a realization beyond the faults, blame or condemnation into a oneness of love. Each experience is the ability to learn from a mistake and transform life into a better one. This change needs to occur, thereby eliminating the past influences; wisdom is learned from the experience. Just the immediate action of a child or adult is not the complete story.

My experience brought understanding of the dynamics involved at an age I could put the dots together; it has developed into a blessing. I am fortunate to have had the ability to raise my consciousness into maturity, while understanding the emotional process and dynamics from my teaching and counseling background. *Knowing the truth* does set you free. That is a form of innocence.

When our focus is in the Realm of the Spirit, rather than the worldly life of tangible objects or the ego's influence**, our new focus is about how can I be helpful, contribute or be of service to others. This is the kingdom — a higher consciousness of unconditional love. "Ye are of God, little children, and have overcome them: because greater is he that is in you, than he that is in the world." 1 John 4:4

Our Father, which is in heaven, is our spiritual father and in all of us, no matter what our age. That consciousness is our innocence. Everyone is the little child as a humble, modest person without blame when we raise into unconditional love like Jesus. At this new stage of growth, we experience a new life of Christ Consciousness. "I have said, 'Ye are Gods; and all of you are children of the most High." Psalms 82:6

* *Paradigm Busters, Reveal the Real You,* Marilyn L. Redmond, Mithra Publishing, 2016. Available at Amazon.com

** *The Real Meaning of 2012, A New Paradigm Bringing Heaven to Earth,* Marilyn l. Redmond, Dreamtime Press, 2014. Available at Amazon.com

The Innocence of Childhood

A Spiritual Master Lives in Christ Consciousness

Christ Consciousness is attainable by everyone. It is becoming conscious of having mastery over your mindset and feelings while in the higher dimension of unconditional love. You have mastered your emotions and emote unconditional love.

In the Bible, the casting out from the "Garden of Eden" was essentially a gift because death, reincarnation and karma are all intended to teach us to move away from the physical world of darkness toward our true nature of the light within. There have been people who have grown into a higher consciousness of unconditional love beyond the material world. They are called masters.

They mastered their emotions through the mystery schools with initiations. Those that have passed the initiations are able to dwell in the fifth dimension. Rather than reacting in fear, anger and resentment, they rose above their lower vibrations into energy that vibrates into maturity or adulthood. Jesus is the most familiar master. Some other known masters are Confucius, Gabriel, Kuthumi, Krishna and St Germain.

Our society has been in dark, low energy of childish behaviors from fear for thousands of years. For many years, parts of our society have proclaimed pessimism, doubt and lack of trust. The news, violence, movies, videos, games, medicine, and climatic traumas have continued to condition society with fear.

Light is shining brighter on the planet today because of the Photon Belt. You can turn on an inner light and see truth. When you were a child, your parent turned on the light to show you there is no bogie man under the bed. It is time to turn on God's

177

light to shine and show you that love is always there when the darkness leaves.

We have been led to believe only one person was able to rise above the ego, devil, or our lower nature of darkness and fears. However, the real story is that we are all born with the Christ consciousness. Christmas is the renewal of knowing we all have that spirit within. It is our job to reveal that spirit that has been covered by past calamity, abuse and trauma in our lives, known as karma. Jesus came to overcome the darkness from negative thinking, behaviors, and long-ago. He came to show us that we can move into the light and love of God, too. We can ascend into a higher consciousness of unconditional love of the fifth dimension. Jesus is our pattern, according to Edgar Cayce, the most documented psychic of the twentieth century and the Father of Holistic Health.

When trusting the universe to support us in all things, we too can move into heaven on earth or beyond the negativity and abusive past motivated from our ego. Raising our consciousness takes numerous lives to accomplish. The Bible deleted most of the passages of the earlier lives of Jesus and his growth into Christhood or Christ Consciousness. According to Cayce, Jesus was the man who attained complete "at-one-ment" and human-divine unity and therefore became the "Christ." When Jesus received the sign of the dove at his baptism, this was the recognition of his rising into the consciousness of the Christ.

The planet has been in third dimension of right and wrong, good and bad, and criticism and judgment. Moving higher is often described as a ladder. While growing into a higher consciousness, your realization grows into more clarity through the Fourth Dimension and into the Fifth Dimension.

A human being who has taken the appropriate actions of

Initiation is capable of dwelling in the Fifth Dimension of living in a higher reality of total love. Cayce described the Christ soul as the impelling force and core of truth behind all religions that teach "God is One." This level of awareness is characterized by cooperation, harmony and oneness, rather than competition, conflict and fear.

"The whole essence of truth *cannot be transmitted from mouth to ear*. Nor can any pen describe it, not even that of the recording Angel, unless man finds the answer in the sanctuary of his own heart, in the innermost depths of his divine intuitions." *The Secret Doctrine* 2:516. This shows that it is experience and not knowledge that transports us into a higher consciousness of the presence of God, which comes through faith. " 'I and my Father are one.'

"Then they took up stones again to stone him. Jesus answered them, 'Many good works have I shown you from my Father; for which of these do you stone me?' They answered him, saying, 'For a good work we stone you not; but for blasphemy; and because that you, being a man, make yourself God.' Jesus answered them, 'Is it not written in your law: I said you are gods?'" — John 10:30-34. This response was to support the teaching that God dwells within all human beings. *The Great Reality* is deep within. When we achieve that level of consciousness, we have moved beyond the material world into the Realm of Spirit. We feel our inner goodness.

Attributes of Christ Consciousness

1. Harmony

We are all in oneness. There is only All That Is. As a spiritual master, you know that everything is one spiritual energy. Separation is a delusion because everything is a part of the whole, interconnected, and interdependent. Therefore, the action taken affects others and ultimately everything in the universe. With this understanding, the Golden Rule shows us that, "Do unto others as you would have them do unto you" is saying that what you do to another, you are doing to yourself. As a result, you treat everyone and everything with kindness and thoughtfulness as a basis for life and live in harmony.

2. Forever Tell the Truth

In a higher consciousness, it is not congruent to say something that is not truthful. Speaking from less than truth would not be possible because the lack of truth would be apparent to the listener. This lacks integrity. It alters energy you are sending out and inhibits communication. In addition, denial or lying to yourself is deceiving yourself, and eliminates unity with self. When your words and your actions do not match, there is a discrepancy called lack of honesty. This impedes equality and embracing oneness. When you speak the truth, you take fitting and appropriate action.

3. Actions Match Communication

It takes being trustworthy to have your actions match your words. It is essential to be humble and honest by taking responsibility for a situation. Verify that your actions are constantly reliable with your words. If you cannot match your words later, then it is necessary to face it squarely, talk to those involved, and clear up the situation, quickly.

4. Apply Resolution to What Works

When a highly advanced person sees a less than desirable situation and understands why it exists, they will counter with something that works. Repeating or ignoring what does not work increases the problem. Therefore, educating people to respond in loving solutions is not the typical action; however, it does work. They do not ignore it, deny that it exists, cover it up, or do something that does not address the true problem as many could. In addition, doing nothing is a common lack of response that does not lead to a better way.

5. Avoid Killing Anything

Do not try to protect yourself, which is actually attacking another at a subconscious level, because they will retaliate. The adversary is in pain and hurting. They are projecting out their misery to hurt another, hoping their suffering will leave them. When you send love back to them, they cannot harm you. It is productive to send love and prayers. Love stops the conflict.

The people in your life are playing out a part for you to learn to love your neighbor as yourself. We are all one. Another person is a mirror of yourself; you would be hurting a part of you. As I sent forgiveness, gratitude, compassion, and unconditional love to my abusers, I found that I had grown into maturity. I cannot harm animals or insects. In addition, today when I find spiders, I take them outside.

6. Never Harm the Surroundings

Knowing that the earth is a living soul, we need to love all consciousness. Damaging the environment does not support life. To desecrate anything living is not in alignment with the love of the universe within us all. Preventing the harming of nature precludes the demise of our lives. All nature has the energy of love within every plant, flower and tree. They sustain us. An evolved individual promotes environmental safeguards to continue our natural settings for future generations.

7. Sharing Means No Ownership

When the first man set foot on the North American continent, the indigenous Indians had no concept of ownership of the land. It was from the Great Spirit and they were the stewards. They simply managed the land, animals, and fished for the tribe. It was the Europeans and other settlers that brought the concept of ownership with them. When years later, the Indians were forced to sign a treaty to stay in a designated area, or reservation, they became prisoners on their own land put in their trust, which Spirit had given them for their benefit and needs.

People became greedy and wanted power by owning land. Sadly, it was at the expense of those who could not afford or fight for land ownership. A concept that is based in competition and self glory is producing a society of lack for the greater population. If there were sharing, would there be a deficiency?

A mature person shares and finds more to give. The universe always has supported our needs and always will. "The LORD is my shepherd; I shall not want." Psalm 23. There is more than enough for everyone, if you see the whole picture. Being selfish stops love flowing and being selfless allows love to flow everywhere.

8. Unity Replaces Competition

Unity is not a new idea. Moving beyond competition into cooperation is productive. When we grow into a state of joining, our wellbeing expands. The song, "The Brotherhood of Man," brings us together as sung by Robert Morse in the musical show, "How to Succeed in Business." The Youngbloods, The Dave Clark Five, and Jefferson Airplane all sing, "C'mon people now, smile on your brother, everybody get together and try and love one another right now."

"If we have no peace, it is because we have forgotten that we belong to each other," said Mother Teresa. In addition, the Bible tells us the same thing. When we love our neighbor as ourselves, we are in accord. In addition, it says, "Till we all come in the unity of the faith, and of the knowledge of the Son of God, unto a perfect man, unto the measure of the stature of the fullness of Christ:." Ephesians 4:13

Life is not about who has the most toys wins, but unity of spirit, which is precious and divine. Our inner lives are the real test to a mature person living in the light of the universe. Joining heart to heart is love. It is what you do not see that makes the person.

9. Replace Punishment with Compassion

When a person acts out in pain, it is a cry for help, according to *A Course in Miracles*. Justice and punishment are a reaction and misunderstanding of people's actions. Only love heals, and this is the answer to restore health and sanity to a wounded person. Moving beyond the principle of punishment is spiritual. Seeing that love transforms is virtuous and moral. When people use the Golden Rule, *do unto others as you would have them do unto you*, there is no need for punishment. Education, support, and loving therapy to heal, provide the necessary tools for transforming a damaged life. With just actions, there is no need for penalty. A healed person acts in the best interest of all and contributes to society. We all encourage this ultimate goal. Love never fails.

10. There is no Lack

There is no death and they live eternally in the spirit of the universe. A master has moved into knowing that they create their own reality. Therefore, they have no fear or lack. Having removed their barriers to accepting the gifts of spirit, there is no shortage. The items needed appear from the invisible world and materialize as needed.

They have mastered their thoughts, words and actions to come from their hearts rather than the fear-based thinking of the ego. They understand that the fullness in their hearts manifests into the material world, and their needs are met from spirit. The verse that brings this together is "My grace is sufficient." 2 Corinthians 12:9. This is called the Creator consciousness versus the victim consciousness. Your prosperity is guaranteed. "But seek ye first the kingdom of God, and his righteousness; and all these things shall be added unto you." Matthew 6:33

A spiritual master is living in the unconditional love of the universe. They know that all matter is merely energy condensed to a slow vibration for materiality. They understand that we are all one in that consciousness and can experience it subjectively. There is no fear of death as we are eternal in spirit, and that spirit manifests for us and in us. Ralph Waldo Emerson said, "The highest revelation is that God is in every man."

Epilogue

My life has amazed me. I did not know I was not living in reality either in my growing up or in my teaching years. It took a terrifying experience so profound to get my attention that I desperately prayed for help because I wanted to live. My life began a new path in faith rather than survival. Little did I know this new focus would lead me to find reality, deep inside and unconditional love in myself, and in the universal energy of love.

I lived as Cinderella most of my life, wanting to be treated fairly and kindly. I ignorantly and blindly served others. The advice from authority and experts was not healthy or productive, as my hell increased. My life going to church was not the answer. Seeking medical doctors and psychiatrists did not help, ultimately. By forgiving the past, I give up my servitude to my ego. Moving into a daily consciousness with my Creator permits me to grow beyond the appearances into the meaning of life.

The label of God from a church definition does not matter. I found my own description of God moved me into the Realm of Spirit. When I began a spiritual path for sobriety, I found the answers for which I was always looking.

All my medical and relationship problems were the manifestations from a lack of stability and a loving basis to my life that flows through me to others. I have moved into my heart, where the consciousness of the universe flows through when I allow it. Love brings health to my body and enhances my life.

My new knowledge not to react from fear, but to respond in love to life's challenges, has paid off in spades. I finally see how my past was not living in the experience of God's presence. The barriers I built to protect me from past harms have now disappeared. Their removal has opened the channel for reality, awareness, and being current in my life.

Leaving the 3rd dimensional material world of duality and the ego's fear is a huge transition. Adjusting to a life in love is an adventure. Today I am part of this wonderful world of love and appreciate being happy, joyous and free to be myself. I enjoy the moment and each day has new gifts for me. Moving into the Fifth Dimension of a consciousness of unconditional love offers me heaven on earth. My new experience is living in the everlasting love of reality.

Blessings, Marilyn

Appendix

Chart of Ascending Energies

Rev. Marilyn L. Redmond
BA, CHT, IBRT

Marilyn Redmond is a pioneer, innovative warrior and spiritual wayshower in restoring traumatic lives, healing emotional causes of illness and releasing negative energy. The answers to life are no longer a mystery. Her understanding and wisdom of the human dilemma and the solutions will work for you, too.

Marilyn became a minister to do spiritual counseling, channeling, and to give psychic readings. She is a member of the International Board of Regression Therapy, American Board of Hypnotherapy, and lifetime member of Edgar Cayce's Association for Research and Enlightenment. Redmond teaches in colleges, wellness centers and for metaphysical groups. Her radio show, "Marilyn's Solutions," interviews, and TV appearances are big successes. Join her new live call in radio show, "Love Never Fails," on Tuesday afternoons at 3:00 PM Pacific Time, 866-451-1451.

- Web site: Angelicasgifts.com
- Blog is marilynredmondbooks.blogspot.com
- See her videos for interviews, lectures, and channeling on YouTube at www.youtube.com/user/puyallup98372.
- You can read Marilyn's international monthly column on http://www.thesussexnewspaper.com
- She is available for speaking, interviews, seminars, individual counseling, regression therapy, and personal psychic readings.
- She does inspirational art of your personal guardian angels, portraits of family and pets, and other artistic paintings, cards and gifts by commission.
- Books at http://www.amazon.com/Marilyn-Redmond/ e/B0069WIKDC
- Her lectures, interviews and spiritual information can be found on You Tube at https://www.youtube.com/ user/puyallup98372/videod?shelf_id=48view=08sort=dd

Contact her at *marilyn@angelicasgifts.com* for readings and portraits.

Publications by Marilyn L. Redmond

Books

Road to Success, Earth Star Publications, © 2017
Paradigm Busters, Reveal the Real You, Mithra Publishing, © 2016
The Real Meaning of 2012, A New Paradigm for Bringing Heaven to Earth, Dreamtime Press, © 2014
Roses Have Thorns; Encouragement on Evolving from Pain to Joy— Poetry, Kaleidoscope Press, © 1999

E-Books on Amazon.com

Vasanas, The Gifts That Show Us the Way
Incest, Love Heals the Soul
All Time Victim, Domestic Violence
Spiritual Alignment, Are You Ready for 2012
Peace on Earth, Finding Your New Life

Anthologies — Prose

The Book of Amazing People, "What a Dream!" © 2017
  Mithra Publishing and Athena Publishing
The Book of Success, "New Glasses Bring Success," © 2015
  http://mithrapublishing.com/product/the-book-of-success
Hidden Success, "Beyond the Barriers to Success," © 2016
  http://mithrapublishing.com
Walking Your Life, "I Wanted to Live," © 2015
  http://mithrapublishing.com
Grand-Stories, Ernie Wendell, Friendly Oaks Publications, pp. 60-61
  © 2000
Recovery, "Pygmalion," an anthology, John M. Daniel, Editor,
  © 1994.

Published Poetry Single and Anthologies

- "Peace At Last," Poetry.com © 2012
  http://poetry.com/poems/149784?selected=reviews#comments
- "My-Gala-Celebration," http://poetry.com/poems/145132
- "The-Light-of-Truth," http://poetry.com/poems/85867
- "VISION-A NEW ME," *Spiritually Speaking,* © 2006
- "Love," *First Word Bulletin,* Spain © 1997
- "Parade of Dreams," *First Word Bulletin,* Spain, © 1997.
- "Forever Christmas," *First Word Bulletin,* Spain © 1995
- "Leaving Home," *Newscaper,* Tacoma Writer Club, ©1994

- *When We Were Young: Childhood,* A Community of Voices, poem, ©2000
- *When We Were Young: Adulthood,* A Community of Voices, poem © 2000
- *Hot Dog, A Community of Voices,* art, Santa Barbara Writers, © 1999
- *Winging It With Words,* A Community of Voices, poem and art, Santa Barbara Writers © 1997
- *Poetry* — The Twenty-fourth Annual SFWC, © 1996
- *Silence Captured Still,* Tacoma Writers Club, © 1994
- "Love," *Our World's Most Treasured Poems,* World of Poetry Press, © 1991

Made in the USA
Middletown, DE
12 March 2022